HOSPITALITY MANAGEMENT: AVOIDING LEGAL PITFALLS

JON P. McCONNELL, J. D.
AND
LOTHAR A. KRECK, PH. D

Jule Wilkinson, Editor

CAHNERS BOOKS, INC.
221 Columbus Ave., Boston, Massachusetts 02116
Publishers of Institutions/VF Magazine

0-8436-2064-1

To Our Families

Contents

Preface

The purpose of this text is to present a broad outline of the more important legal problems facing the operator and manager in the hospitality industry. It is written for the practicing manager of a hotel, motel, foodservice operation, or club, as well as the owner or franchisee of a hospitality operation, the trainee, and the student of hospitality management. The purpose of this text is to focus attention on concrete management policies that may be taken to minimize the danger of legal liability.

The authors have tried to present some of the ramifications of the law as it applies to any one of the many subjects discussed. One way of viewing the law, at least when dealing with fairly well-defined areas such as are discussed below, might be as a system of general rules, to which there are usually exceptions and, often, further exceptions to the exceptions. We will deal only with general rules, and, perhaps, *some* exceptions. Our hope is that this sort of treatment will serve as a guide to intelligent planning in order to avoid liability, even if it will not infallibly tell the operator or manager whether he is liable after some particular event has occurred.

This text is *not* intended to be a comprehensive legal guide with solutions to all legal problems. That is for your lawyer. This discussion is intended to provide a basis for planning preventive actions. We hope that it will suggest areas where policies should be thought through, probably with the aid of an attorney, for the purpose of avoiding future legal entanglement. Very likely, the reader will identify problem areas within his own operation that he had not previously suspected of presenting a danger. If we succeed in helping him spot them, we have achieved our goal.

We have used many examples and actual cases to underline our points. Since we assumed that our readers would not be interested in the legal arguments which preceded the judgments, as pointed out above, we have abstained from footnoting. However, we have added pertinent comments at the end of the cases. These appear in italics preceded by a ✱.

One of the authors of this text has a background in the management of hospitality operations; the other, in law. We hope, therefore, that we can communicate effectively as practitioners to practitioners.

We wish to extend our appreciation to Dr. John H. Rudd, Professor of Hotel Administration at the University of Nevada at Las Vegas, and Dr. Alan S. Jeffrey, Executive Director, Education Institute of the American Hotel-Motel Association, East Lansing, Michigan.

Both of these scholars diligently studied our manuscript and provided many helpful suggestions. Such errors as may be found herein are entirely our own responsibility.

Jon P. McConnell
Lothar A. Kreck

HOSPITALITY MANAGEMENT: AVOIDING LEGAL PITFALLS

CHAPTER 1

The Legal System

Introduction

ANY LEGAL SYSTEM provides, among other things, a means by which certain rights and duties are defined. When these rights and duties are violated, a legal remedy, usually an award of money damages, is imposed. In the United States, as elsewhere, this system is not perfect. For one thing, attorneys do require fees, and frequently, a wrong is too small to justify the cost of starting a law suit.

Even a moderate wrong might involve extensive legal fees, in which case the pursuit of damages may not be worth the effort. Moreover, there is the question of proof. If a wrong cannot be proved with a fair degree of clarity, there is no point in bringing suit.[1] Finally, the party sued may have no assets. An award of damages merely allows the winner to collect, if he can, from the assets of the other party. We no longer have debtors' prisons, so if the party sued has no assets,

---

1. See Glossary for explanation of terms.

about all that can be done is to wait and hope that he will accumulate some property.

Despite these limitations, our legal system is a matter of importance to the business world, including the hospitality industry. Very frequently, when a legal wrong occurs, the wronged party does elect to bring suit, succeeds in his action, and collects an award of damages.

Some discussion of the terms and procedures used in our legal system is necessary for an understanding of the pages that follow.

The party who believes himself to have been wronged and thereby files suit is the plaintiff. The party who is alleged to have committed a wrong and who is being sued is the defendant. The court in which a suit is initially filed in important cases is the trial court. This is merely a descriptive term, not the term used in any particular state. This court is known by a wide variety of names—Superior Court, District Court, County Court, for example. The common denominator is that this court has unlimited jurisdiction, meaning that suit may be brought for any amount and that, usually, either party is entitled to a jury trial.

All states have appellate courts, where a decision of the trial court may be appealed, though appeal is more limited than commonly supposed. Essentially, only errors of law committed by the judge may be the basis for reversal or retrial. The facts of a case are established at the trial court by the jury or, if the parties agree not to have a jury, by the judge.

Most suits involving the hospitality industry arise as questions of state law. Usually, therefore, such suits will be heard in state courts. Occasionally, the federal courts may be involved. The trial court at the federal level is the Federal District Court, and the first appellate court is the Circuit Court of Appeals.

The final award made by a court to a successful plaintiff is termed a judgment. As noted above, a judgment is not self-enforcing, but requires that money or property of the defendant be seized and liquidated, providing that the defendant will not pay short of such action, though often he will.

Many suits are brought for smaller amounts in courts of limited jurisdiction. These have various names, for example, Justice Court and Court of Small Claims. These courts differ from the trial court in that there is some absolute maximum above which a plaintiff may not recover. Moreover, a jury trial is not always provided for and, in practice, is rare because frequently the attorneys do not wish to bother with the increased time and formality a jury trial requires.

Most legal issues involving the hotel, motel, or foodservice manager concern the area of law known either as contract or tort. Essentially, a contract is an agreement made between two parties in which each gives up something to the other, and which the law recognizes as legally binding. If one party breaks a contract, the other party may sue to recover such damages as may reasonably be attributed to that breach.

Torts consist of an odd bag of acts recognized as wrong, but which are not based upon any agreement and are, therefore, distinguished from contract. It is easier to enumerate well-known torts than it is to define common denominators. Assault and battery, libel and slander, and negligence are examples. These are considered later in this text.

Criminal Law and Civil Law

There are two major subdivisions of the law. One is the *criminal law,* which involves prosecution brought, in an effort to regulate society, by the state for commission of criminal acts. Successful prosecution will normally result in fine or imprisonment with the objectives of deterring others from like offenses, punishing offenders, and rehabilitating them. About the only crimes discussed in these pages are those of defrauding the innkeeper and writing bad checks.

Most of this text is concerned with the *civil law,* which refers to private lawsuits between two parties, usually to secure an award of money to compensate for a loss or injury. Tort and contract are both areas of the civil law, and both are important to the manager of the hospitality operation.

Common Law and Statute

Although most of the chapters that follow deal with the question "What is the law?" (in some cases this question cannot be clearly answered, because the law varies from state to state), it is also useful to know from where a rule of law has derived.

There are two primary sources of law in the United States. The first of these is common law. Although common law is exceedingly important, it is possible that the reader may not be familiar with this source of law if he is not familiar with legal matters. Common law is derived entirely from decisions of our appellate courts. Common law is not enacted by our state or federal legislatures. It traces its origin to decisions of English courts made during medieval days. These decisions were used as precedents in later cases. English law was brought to the United States, and after the states became separate entities, their appellate courts continued to rely upon these and their own precedents, until today each state has its own body of common law, traceable back to precedents from English law.

Occasionally, a state appellate court may, for good reason, depart from the traditional rule of the common law in order to bring the law into harmony with modern conditions. Such a departure will merely constitute a new rule of that state's common law. The distinguishing feature of common law is that it is based on judicial decision, not on an act of the state legislature.

Most of the rules of tort, contract, and property discussed in the following chapters are based upon state common law. Almost all of the law of innkeepers was developed generations ago as part of English common law, then brought to this country.

Legislation

The common law may be modified any time a majority of the legislators of a state feel so inclined, merely by the passage of an act in the state legislature. Many rules discussed in the following chapters are affected by legislation; for example, the innkeepers' lien, crimes against innkeepers, and bad checks are governed by legislation in almost every state. Any time legislation and the common law are in conflict, legislation will control. Enacting legislation is a rapid and definitive way of changing the law.

A particular bit of legislation is referred to as a statute. Both terms are used in the chapters that follow.

CHAPTER 2

Legal Issues and the Hospitality Industry

Introduction

IN UNDERTAKING a discussion of legal liability in the hospitality industry, two things must be accomplished at the outset. First, we must make it clear exactly what forms of business enterprises we are including within the term, hospitality operation, and, second, we must describe the extent to which the nature of legal problems varies among different forms of hospitality operation.

The Inn

In the chapters that follow we will use the term *inn* in reference to either a hotel or motel because normally the legal liability of the two is identical. Moreover, many large, modern, "motels" provide all the services of the modern hotel and cannot logically be distinguished from the traditional hotel at all, except, perhaps, in providing more convenient parking than usual. In many cases, it is impossible to determine whether an establishment should be classified as motel or hotel. However, in those few instances where there has traditionally been a difference in the law between the two we will specify whether we are referring to hotel or motel.

But what is an inn? Essentially we mean an enterprise which publicly holds itself out to accommodate guests, usually travellers, for periods of short duration. Such an enterprise usually describes itself as a hotel or motel, and the fact that it does so is some evidence that it is legally an inn. That it provides maid service, room service, and other services for short-term travellers is additional evidence that an enterprise is an inn.

A number of important legal consequences flow from the fact of being an inn. Many of these are explored in greater detail in succeeding chapters, and some are mentioned only in this discussion.

Duty of Innkeeper to Accept All Persons

In the first place, if an establishment holds itself out to be an inn, and the facts appear to indicate that it is, the inn owes a duty to accommodate all well-comported persons for its services. The reasons for this are based upon history. In medieval England, travellers had nowhere to go to be safe at night except to an inn, and if they were refused entrance, their very lives were in danger. Of course, this obligation of the inn applies only if there are vacant rooms available.

Violation by the innkeeper of this legally imposed duty could give rise to either criminal or civil liability in many states. Because the obligation of the innkeeper to accommodate is imposed upon him as a matter of law and applies even to those who could normally avoid contracts, notably minors, the question arises: is there a contract between innkeeper and guest, once the latter has agreed to take accommodations? The best reasoning appears to support the proposition that there *is* a contract, and that even if a confirmed reservation is made in advance, the reservation will be an enforceable contract. Therefore, either party could successfully sue if the other violates his agreement. But, since the obligation to provide accommodations is also imposed by law, probably even a minor could be held to this contract.

TABLE 1

ROOM NO.					DEPART DATE	RATE

GUEST REGISTRATION
PLEASE PRINT

NO. IN PARTY
ADS. | CHILD.

LAST NAME	FIRST	INITIAL

HOME ADDRESS: SIGNATURE
STREET

CITY   STATE   ZIP

FIRM

MAKE OF CAR	LICENSE NO.	STATE

ON CHECKING OUT MY ACCOUNT WILL BE HANDLED BY:

☐ CASH   ☐ CHECK

☐ CREDIT CARD – KIND_____NO._____

NOTICE TO GUESTS
THIS PROPERTY IS PRIVATELY OWNED AND THE MANAGEMENT RESERVES THE
RIGHT TO REFUSE SERVICES TO ANYONE, AND WILL NOT BE RESPONSIBLE FOR
ACCIDENTS OR INJURY TO GUESTS. THE MANAGEMENT PROVIDES A SAFE IN
THE OFFICE AND CAN NOT BE RESPONSIBLE FOR VALUABLES UNLESS THE
GUEST CHECKS THEM AT THE OFFICE.

REMARKS

CLERK'S INITIAL   TIME CHECKED IN

069501

The statement on the above registration card dealing with the refusal of service, presently used in a hospitality operation in the state of Washington, is clearly void and cannot be enforced by the innkeeper.

Who Is Not a Well-Comported Person?

Who is and who is not a well-comported person? Essentially this is a matter of common sense. However, some frequently encountered problems can be dealt with specifically. Guests can be required to meet house rules stating that they wear shirts and shoes. Those persons who are, by ordinary standards, considered to be of bad reputation, may be excluded. Conduct reasonably leading to the conclusion that persons, unknown to the management, are of ill repute will also be a basis whereby they may be excluded. A customer entertaining or attempting to entertain women of ill repute in his room may be excluded.[1] The same considerations would obtain in the case of one homosexual entertaining another homosexual.[2]

Drunkenness is possibly the most frequently encountered basis for denying admittance to an applicant for the services of an inn, and it is well established that this alone is sufficient. A pattern of violence or conduct appearing to threaten either the safety of the innkeeper or his other guests would constitute an independent ground for barring a person, whether this condition was coupled with drunkenness or not.

loophole Possession of pets that might disturb other guests or damage property is a sufficient reason for denying admittance.

The above situations represent only some of the more obvious and frequently encountered situations. In general, the maxim is true, that if a guest for any reason would disturb other guests or endanger persons or property of management, exclusion of the person will be proper. One last fact should be mentioned. Damages based on improper exclusion from an inn are rarely large, and, possibly because of the fact that costs of suit are high compared to expected recovery, there do not appear to be large numbers of suits brought on this basis.

When is Eviction From the Premises Justified?

In general, a guest may be evicted from his quarters for the same reasons that he might have been denied accommodations in the first place. In addition to these reasons, which for the most part involve misconduct, the guest may be evicted

---

1. Recognizing the more liberal code of sexual ethics that has come about in recent years, many inns go to some pains to avoid asking whether a couple is married. Generally, well-behaved unmarried couples probably do not bring disgrace upon the inn, at least in the more liberal regions of the country, notably the East and West Coasts and large Midwestern cities.

2. Many of these areas are obviously delicate and involve a danger of law suits based on defamation which is explored in chapter 3. In case of any doubt, the lesser danger is usually to accept a party, rather than to make accusations which cannot be proved.

for failure to pay his bill as agreed. He may also be locked out of his quarters for these reasons, and, if he is in arrears, the innkeeper's lien may be imposed upon his belongings. This subject is discussed more extensively in chapter 8. In order to successfully lock out a guest, it will probably be necessary to change the lock in his absence so that the guest will be forced to seek out the manager to discuss the situation.

House Rules

In determining whether or not an inn has proper justification for either denying accommodations to an applicant, evicting him, or locking him out, it is proper to consider any house rules which a particular inn may have adopted. Such rules cannot be completely arbitrary, but must have some reasonable relationship to the harmony, convenience, or security of the inn. As long as such rules are reasonable, they may be enforced by management. House rules should be posted in public places or, preferably, in each room so that guests may be apprised of them. It is a good idea for management to devise and post these house rules, if only to make more explicit the vague standard that guests must comport themselves in a reasonable manner.

Public Accommodation Law

At the present time it is illegal to refuse public accommodations which involve interstate commerce (which would include virtually every inn and restaurant) on the basis of race, color, religion, or national origin. Also, many states have similar laws that apply, regardless of interstate commerce. (While possibly an extended discussion of this point could be included, the basic rule is so simple that it is doubtful that much elaboration is necessary. The rule is: do not deny the use of your facilities for reasons of race, color, religion, or national origin. If there is some special reason that you may wish to do so, consult your attorney in advance to see whether you operate under some special exception. (Some exceptions would be private clubs or an operation not in interstate commerce that is also in a state lacking a state antidiscrimination law.)

Other Obligations of the Innkeeper

Aside from the legally imposed duty to receive the guest and the contractually imposed duty to make good on confirmed reservations, the innkeeper has other obligations. There is a duty to extend courteous treatment to the guest, and, accordingly, the inn may be held liable in damages for insult or abusive language directed at the guest. To our knowledge, this is the only instance in American law where mere offensive language, which does not amount to defamation, as discussed in chapter 3, can be the basis for recovery of damages. This liability is considered a logical extension of the obligation of the innkeeper to care for his guest.

The guest is also entitled to reasonable privacy in his accommodations. Although the innkeeper has the right of reasonable access to the guest's room for legitimate purposes, such as cleaning, such activities as conducting an unwarranted search of the premises or bursting in to question about some alleged criminal activity or past debt could be the basis for recovery of damages by the guest.

The innkeeper is an insurer of the property of the guest at common law, meaning that in the event of loss the innkeeper is usually liable. This liability of the innkeeper has been widely modified by statute. The entire question is explored in detail in chapter 5.

The above discussion is intended to summarize the instances in which the obligations of the inn are unique. On the other hand, there is probably only one respect in which the obligation of the restaurant or other foodservice operation is unusual, though even this is not unique. There is an implied warranty, which might be described as an unstated and even unintended guarantee imposed as a matter of law, that all food served will be fit to eat. The warranty would be broken if foreign substances, such as a rock, resulted in a broken tooth; spoilage produced nausea; or contaminants, such as insecticide, produced illness. Obviously, restaurants must impose very tight controls over their procedures in order to be free from suits based on impure food.

Otherwise, restaurants, unlike inns, have no particular forms of legal liability that are not shared by most other forms of business. Restaurants need not accommodate all well-comported applicants.[1] In fact, they may, and sometimes do, impose special requirements for admittance. As is discussed in chapter 4, restaurants and hotels alike are liable for negligent

---

1. They are, of course, subject to the federal and state anti-discrimination laws discussed earlier.

injury to their patrons, but so is any other business. Restaurants are not liable for insult or abusive language to their guests, though hopefully they will not treat their patrons in that fashion. Both restaurants and inns are liable for defamation, assault and battery, and false imprisonment and these torts are treated in chapter 3.

The restaurant is not an insurer of its guest's property as is an inn. The liability the restaurant does incur is discussed in chapter 5. Both restaurants and inns will be liable on their contracts. This subject is discussed in chapter 6.

Finally, the obligations imposed by the federal government under the Labor Management Relations Act, under the Equal Employment Practices Act and allied legislation, and under the Occupational Safety and Health Act naturally apply to both restaurant and inn. These are considered in chapters 11, 12, and 13.

CASE

HOBSON v. YORK STUDIOS, INC.
(NEW YORK 1955) 145 N. Y. S. 2d 162

WAHL, J.: The plaintiffs, Raymond S. Hobson, a Negro, and his wife, a white woman, sue for statutory redress under Section 41 of the Civil Rights Law. They allege that when they applied for a room at the defendant's hotel, they were rejected by reason of their race and the sought public accommodations refused to them on that ground alone.

Section 40 of the Civil Rights Law, speaking of "public accommodations," insofar as applicable here, reads as follows:

"No person, being the owner, lessee, proprietor, manager, superintendent, agent or employee of any such place shall directly or indirectly refuse, withhold from or deny to any person any of the accommodations, advantages, facilities or privileges thereof, . . . on account of race, creed, color or national origin."

The answer of the defendant is, in substance, a general denial and it disclaims any violation of the plaintiffs' civil rights.

The plaintiffs' testimony shows that on May 6, 1953, Mrs. Hobson, a white person, saw a sign on the defendant's hotel stating that a vacancy existed. She went in to seek lodging for herself and her husband. She was alone at the time. The desk clerk, a Mrs. Raleigh, showed Mrs. Hobson Room 62-F, accepted a deposit of $5 and gave Mrs. Hobson a receipt, while reserving the room for both plaintiffs.

The next day, both plaintiffs returned to the defendant's hotel to claim their reservation and pay the balance due. Only Mr. Hobson spoke to the desk clerk, showing the receipt for the reservation. The desk clerk looked at the Hobsons and demanded proof of identification and of the marriage. At that point, an elevator man spoke to the desk clerk, who called him aside, where they had a whispered conversation, after which the desk clerk told Mr. Hobson that the hotel did not want "white and colored" living together in view of the tendency of another interracial couple, who had resided there previously, to fight all the time. . . .

The testimony offered by the defendant through Mrs. Raleigh, the desk clerk, did not dispute that Rose Hobson, a white woman, made the reservation for the room, left a deposit and stated that she would return the next day with her husband for the room. Mrs. Raleigh's testimony differs from that of the plaintiffs as to the reason why the room was refused. She says that the Negro plaintiff returned to the hotel alone with the receipt which had been given his wife. She states that when she demanded identification and proof of marriage, Mr. Hobson became abusive and offensive.

I have accepted the testimony of the plaintiffs, seemingly respectable and worthy citizens, and I am convinced that both of them were discriminated against because of their race. The post litem contention that Mr. Hobson was offensive and abusive and that that was the basis of the refusal to give the plaintiffs accommodations is not convincing, nor was it pleaded as a matter of affirmative defense. It is natural that a defendant accused of racial discrimination will seek avoidance of statutory penalties therefor through "explanations" . . . .

Since no corporate officer of the defendant testified, it does not appear that the defendant gave any instructions to its desk clerk not to discriminate racially. If nothing was said to employees about refusing admission to persons of the colored race, then the acts of the desk clerk are chargeable to the corporation. Once the accusation is made of a racial rejection by a place of public accommodation, a corporate defendant is bound to come forward with proof that the discrimination which is offensive to the statute has been forbidden by specific instructions to corporate employees. On this point the defendant elected to remain mute.

I now come to an aspect of this case which is not free of difficulty: If the white plaintiff, Rose Hobson, was discriminated against because of her race, may she be given relief under the Civil Rights Law? In the search for an answer to this question, it is idle to urge a strict and inflexible construction of the law simply because it is penal in nature. A liberal intent conceived the statute. The proper office of civil rights legislation is to search out hostility to our public policy and apply the proper remedy. Certain it is that:

"Section 40 of the Civil Rights Law prohibits discrimination against any person by reason of race, color or religion. It is remedial statute and must be liberally construed."

The words "any person," when given their usual meanings, must include protection for white persons as well as Negroes who are rejected because of race. To all but the naive, it is clear that a white woman may be the butt of a racial discrimination because she has elected to marry a Negro. I am convinced that both plaintiffs were rejected by the defendant because Mr. Hobson is a Negro and his wife is a white woman. Such a refusal, as applied to Mrs. Hobson, is a rejection of her because of her color. Unless "direct" and "indirect" discriminations are to mean nothing in the law, a white plaintiff must receive equal protection with her Negro husband . . . .

The modern view of New York's civil rights legislation is found in the acute insight of Mr. Justice Bijur's dissenting opinion in Cohn v. Goldgraben, supra. There, a colored waiter in the defendant's restaurant located in Harlem, claimed he could not serve a "colored and white person together." The white person so rejected, sued. After discussing the admonition of Section 40 of the Civil Rights Law against direct or indirect refusal of accommodations on account of race, Judge Bijur went on to say . . .

"It seems to me to be clear that plaintiff was, on the occasion in question, denied the privileges of defendant's restaurant because he was white. The defendant virtually said to plaintiff: 'If you were colored and came here with

Williams (the man she was with), you would be served; but being white, we will not serve you.' "

Judge Bijur would have given the white plaintiff relief under the Civil Rights Law. The cited amendments to the Executive Law make it clear today that any person discriminated against because of color, or race, whether directly or indirectly, is entitled to invoke the statute.

In effect, what the defendant's desk clerk said to Mrs. Hobson was that if she had been married to a white man, her reservation for a room would have been honored. If the rejection was based upon some private theory of "social acceptability," where Negroes and whites are in intimate association, it is still offensive to the law.

The credible testimony confirms a racial discrimination against each of the plaintiffs. . . .

For all the foregoing reasons, I direct that the plaintiffs have judgment against the defendant in the amount of $100 each.

✻ *As stated earlier in this chapter, there is presently a federal statute prohibiting discrimination on the basis of race, color, religion, or national origin in establishments related to travel, such as hotels, motels, restaurants, and even movie theatres. There are also statutes in many states prohibiting similar forms of discrimination, in many instances by any business dealing with the public.*

This case involved a state statute. Almost always in a case of this sort, the defendant argues that some valid reason other than race was the reason for the exclusion. It is, of course, conceivable that in some instances some other reason might be the basis for excluding a person of minority race from an inn. Members of a minority race or religion, together with everyone else, may be excluded if they do not meet the standard of the well-comported person.

Whether a person was excluded because of his race or religion or because he was not a well-comported person is a question of fact to be determined by a jury. Whenever a person is excluded on the basis of not being a well-comported person, and especially if that person is of a racial or religious minority, it is important that the clerk or other representative of the hospitality establishment jot down a record of the facts and circumstances that caused the person to be denied admittance.

This record will be helpful in justifying the establishment's position, should the matter subsequently go to court.

CASE

DOLD v. OUTRIGGER HOTEL
(HAWAII 1972)
(501 P 2d 368)

KOBAYASHI, JUSTICE: This is an appeal by the plaintiffs, Mr. and Mrs. D. F. Dold and Mr. and Mrs. Leo Manthei, from a judgment in their favor. Plaintiffs' amended complaint prayed for actual and punitive damages and alleged three counts for recovery, breach of contract, fraud, and breach of an innkeeper's duty to accommodate guests. (Count II for fraud was voluntarily dismissed at trial.) Though the judgment was favorable to them, the plaintiffs contend that the trial judge erred in not allowing an instruction on the issue of punitive damages. This is the issue before the court.

FACTS

The plaintiffs, mainland residents, arranged for hotel accommodations from February 18 to February 23, 1968, through the American Express Company, the agent of the defendant, Outrigger Hotel, hereinafter referred to as "Outrigger." Hawaii Hotels Operating Company, Ltd., managed and operated the Outrigger. Both are Hawaii corporations.

Upon arrival at the Outrigger on February 18, 1968, the plaintiffs were refused accommodations and were transferred by the Outrigger to another hotel of lesser quality because the Outrigger lacked available space. On February 19 and 20 the plaintiffs again demanded that the defendants honor their reservations but they were again refused.

Though the exact nature of the plaintiffs' reservations is in dispute, the defendants claim that since the plaintiffs made no cash deposit, their reservations were not "confirmed" and for that reason the defendants justifiably dishonored the reservations. Plaintiffs contend that the reservations were "confirmed" as the American Express Company had guaranteed to Outrigger a first night's payment in the event that the plaintiffs did not show up. Further, the plaintiffs claim that this guarantee was in fact the same thing as a cash deposit. Thus, plaintiffs argue that the defendants were under a duty to honor the confirmed reservations. Although the jury awarded $600 to the Dolds and $400 to the Mantheis, it is not known upon which count the recovery was based.

An examination of the record in the instant case shows the following:

(1)   It was the policy of the Outrigger that a reservation was deemed confirmed when either a one night's cash deposit was made or the reservation was made by a booking agent which had established credit with the Outrigger.

(2)   The plaintiffs made their reservations through the American Express Company, which had established credit with the Outrigger.

(3)   In lieu of a cash deposit, the Outrigger accepted American Express Company's guarantee that it would pay the first night's deposit for the plaintiffs.

(4)   On February 18, 1968, the Outrigger referred 29 parties holding reservations at the Outrigger to the Pagoda Hotel which deemed these referrals "overflows."

(5)   On February 18, 1968, the Outrigger had 16 guests who stayed beyond their scheduled date of departure.

(6)   From February 15 to 17 and 19 to 22, 1968, the Outrigger also had more reservations than it could accommodate. Plaintiffs' exhibits Nos. 23 to 29 indicate the number of overflows and referrals of the above-mentioned reservations made by the Outrigger to the Pagoda Hotel on the following dates:

February 15	20 referrals
" 16	20 "
" 17	32 "
" 19	44 "
" 20	9 "
" 21	9 "
" 22	20 "

(7)   Evidence was adduced that the Outrigger made a profit from its referrals to the Pagoda Hotel. Upon advance payment for the rooms to American Ex-

press who in turn paid Outrigger, the plaintiffs were issued coupons representing the prepayment for the accommodations at the Outrigger. On referral by the Outrigger, the Pagoda Hotel's practice was to accept the coupons and bill the Outrigger for the actual cost of the rooms provided. The difference between the coupon's value and the actual value of the accommodations was retained by the Outrigger.

The plaintiffs prevented a profit from being made by the Outrigger by refusing to use the coupons and paying in cash for the less expensive accommodations.

MAY PLAINTIFFS RECOVER PUNITIVE DAMAGES FOR BREACH OF CONTRACT?

The question of whether punitive damages are properly recoverable in an action for breach of contract has not been resolved in this jurisdiction.

In the instant case, on the evidence adduced, the trial court refused to allow an instruction on the issue of punitive damages but permitted an instruction on the issue of emotional distress and disappointment.

In a case involving a similar pattern of overbooking of reservations the court in Wills v. Trans World Airlines, stated that the substantial overselling of confirmed reservations for the period in question was a strong indication that the defendant airline had wantonly precipitated the very circumstances which compelled the removal of excess confirmed passengers from its flights.

In Goo v. Continental Casualty Company, we affirmed the public policy considerations behind the doctrine of punitive damages and acknowledged the fact that some jurisdictions allow a recovery of punitive damages where the breach of contract is accompanied by some type of contemporaneous tortious activity. However, the *Goo* case did not afford the proper factual setting for this court to consider the propriety of an assessment of punitive damages in contract actions.

Various jurisdictions have adopted their own rules regarding the nature of the tortious activity necessary to recover punitive damages in a contract action. Some require that the breach be accompanied by an independent willful tort or by a fraudulent act or by a concurrent breach of a common law duty.

[1, 2] We are of the opinion that the facts of this case do not warrant punitive damages. However, the plaintiffs are not limited to the narrow traditional contractual remedy of out-of-pocket losses alone. We have recognized the fact that certain situations are so disposed as to present a fusion of the doctrines of tort and contract. Though some courts have strained the traditional concept of compensatory damages in contract to include damages for emotional distress and disappointment, we are of the opinion that where a contract is breached in a wanton or reckless manner as to result in a tortious injury, the aggrieved person is entitled to recover in tort. Thus, in addition to damages for out-of-pocket losses, the jury was properly instructed on the issue of damages for emotional distress and disappointment.

MAY PLAINTIFFS RECOVER PUNITIVE DAMAGES FOR BREACH OF AN INNKEEPER'S DUTY TO AC-COMMODATE?

[3-6] We now consider count III of plaintiff's complaint. It has long been recognized that an innkeeper, holding himself out to the public to provide hotel accommodations, is obligated, in the absence of reasonable grounds for refusal, to provide accommodations to all persons upon proper request. This duty traditionally extended to the traveller who presented himself at the inn. However, where the innkeeper's accommodations had been exhausted, the innkeeper could justly refuse to receive an applicant. It is well recognized that punitive damages are recoverable for breach of an innkeeper's duty to his guest where the innkeeper's conduct is deliberate or wanton. We are not aware of any jurisdiction that renders an innkeeper liable on his common law duty to accommodate under the circumstances of this case. Consequently, plaintiffs are not entitled to an instruction on punitive damages on count III of their complaint.

Judgment is affirmed.

* *There is some discussion of tort in this case, and, admittedly, this may be a new term to the reader. Chapters 3 and 4 of this text deal with various torts, but for the moment we*

will confine our discussion to stating that a tort is a wrongful act for which the law allows money damages, and which act is not merely breach of contract.

In this case, the court is holding that even though the act of the inn was a breach of contract, the wanton and reckless conduct in knowingly overbooking reservations amounted practically to a tort.   Consequently, damages beyond those normally available for breach of contract were permitted.

CASE

HARDER v. AUBERGE DES FOUGERES
(NEW YORK 1972)
(338 NYS 2d 356)

PER CURIAM

This is an appeal from an order of the Supreme Court at Special Term, entered March 7, 1972 in Albany County, which granted defendants' motion to dismiss the complaint for failure to state a cause of action.

The first cause of action alleged by appellant states, in part, that respondent "unlawfully, willfully, deliberately, and without just cause, refused to admit or seat plaintiff and his guests for dinner service even though plaintiff and his guests (a) had made a bona fide reservation, (b) requested service, and (c) were ready, willing and able to pay any reasonable charges imposed by defendants for such meal." And further that, "By reason of defendants' actions and failure to furnish plaintiff and his guests with appropriate accommodations in this restaurant, plaintiff and his guests were subjected to great inconvenience, humiliation, and insult and were exposed to public ridicule in the presence of a number of people in such restaurant. As a result of the activities of defendants, its officers, agents, representatives or employees, plaintiff and his guests were forced to leave this restaurant and proceed to another place for their meals. Because of the commotion caused by defendants, plaintiff was injured in his good name and reputation which was absolutely uncalled for and unwarranted . . ."

[1] The complaint must be viewed in the framework of our liberal rules of pleading, and if what is stated is a cause

of action cognizable by the courts of this State, the pleading must be sustained.

At common law a person engaged in a public calling, such as an innkeeper or common carrier, was held to be under a duty to the general public and was obligated to serve, without discrimination, all who sought service. On the other hand, proprietors of private enterprises, such as places of amusement and resort, were under no such obligation, enjoying an absolute power to serve whom they pleased.

[2] The reason for the rule that innkeepers could not refuse service to members of the public was to make travel throughout the King's domain possible. For whatever benefit and purpose the rule once served in ancient times, it has no relevance in the 20th Century, and should not be recognized for the purpose of distinguishing inns from other places of public accommodation. In our view, a restaurant proprietor should be under the same duty as an innkeeper to receive all patrons who present themselves "in a fit condition," unless reasonable cause exists for a refusal to do so.

Moreover, there is some authority indicating that the ancient rule is not well regarded. Blackstone stated that a cause of action would lie against "an inn-keeper, or other victualler" who refused to admit a traveler without cause (3 Blackstone's Comm. Sharswood ed. p. 166), and Judge Cardozo found that a "plaintiff, if wrongfully ejected from . . . [a] cafe, was entitled to recover damages for injury to his feelings as a result of the humiliation." Although in *Morningstar* the plaintiff was a guest in the hotel wherein the cafe from which he was ejected was situated, there is nothing in the opinion to indicate that this was a crucial factor in the court's decision.

[3, 4] Furthermore, a proprietor of an inn or similar establishment, is under a duty to protect his patrons from injury, annoyance, or mistreatment through the acts of his servants or employees. The law imposes an obligation upon him to see that his agents and employees extend courteous and decent treatment to his guests, and holds himself liable in violation of this obligation by the use of insulting and abusive language. For these reasons we conclude that the allegations of the first cause of action adequately plead an intentional tort (59 N. Y. Jr., Torts, ¶12, 22).

The order should be modified, on the law and the facts,

so as to deny the motion to dismiss the first cause of action, and, as so modified, affirmed, without costs.

Order modified, on the law and the facts, so as to deny the motion to dismiss the first cause of action, and, as so modified, affirmed, without costs.

HERLIHY, P. J., GREENBLOTT and KANE, J. J., concur.

SIMONS and REYNOLDS, J. J., dissent and vote to affirm in an opinion by REYNOLDS, J.

REYNOLDS, Justice (dissenting).

We would affirm. The complaint does not state a cause of action under common law or statute. Appellant does not claim or argue a cause of action for an intentional tort. We cannot agree with the dictum discussion which would extend the duty of a hotel owner to that of a restaurant under the case law.

* *This is an unusual case. As we noted earlier, most states do not treat a restaurant in the same fashion as an inn, in the sense that a restaurant is required to accept all well-comported persons.*

There is at least one exception. New York State does require restaurants to accept all well-comported persons. This case is authority for that proposition. There is, of course, the possibility that via the route of common law decision, other states will adopt the New York rule. For the time being, however, one can assume that in the vast majority of states a restaurant may turn away customers it has reason not to serve.

Management Ideas: General Advice[1]

1. Never accept or act on the "legal advice" of a person who is not a lawyer, e.g., a friend or a business associate.

2. Do not assume that you know the law: too many changes occur too fast.

3. When you think that a legal problem has emerged, wait and cool off for 24 hours before you write or sign anything. Also, do not make any verbal statements. Observe the rule of silence.

4. Every contract or agreement should be checked by a lawyer, even those which vary slightly from previous, proven forms.

5. Try everything to avoid a suit. It is less expensive to make concessions.

6. Do not threaten in business situations; you must give the other party a chance to "save face." Otherwise the party might be forced into a suit involving you.

7. It is easier (and less costly) to have serious business disagreements settled by third parties, e.g., the attorneys of the parties who are not emotionally involved in the dispute.

8. Do not get involved in business deals which might involve a chance of legal action. It is too risky and costly.

9. When you ask for legal advice, follow it and do not try to substitute your own ideas. You paid for the advice.

10. Even though you bought insurance protection, this does not mean that you bought full legal protection.

11. Give all the facts concerning a legal problem to your lawyer. Do not withhold anything in the belief that it is outside the problem. The lawyer can only act on what information he has from you.

12. Be very sure that you know the difference between facts and assumptions. In general, facts can be either seen, heard, smelled, or touched. Assumptions are mental constructs not necessarily connected with facts.

13. Do not make any remarks about your competitors' faults. It might be the beginning of a suit for libel or slander.

14. Before the guests depart, try to settle all complaints on the premises by a rebate from, or adjustments to, his account. This not only makes for a satisfied customer, but also mini-

---

1. Many of the presented ideas have appeared in different form in the *Tourist Court Journal*, June, 1964 and April, 1970.

mizes expensive correspondence and costly litigation. Avoiding such suits also results in lower insurance premiums.

15. Below is an example of how to handle the problem of guests' pets.

RESPONSIBILITY DECLARATION*

I, _____,
hereby accept full responsibility and payment for any damages or disturbances incurred by my pet during our stay at the Seattle Doubletree.

_____
Guest's Signature

Date _____   Room No. _____

*Courtesy of Doubletree Inn, Seattle, Washington.

CHAPTER 3

The Intentional Torts and Defamation

Introduction

THIS SECTION INCLUDES a discussion of intentional injury to one person by another, which is known technically as battery, and the threat or offer to commit an intentional injury, which is known as assault. We will also discuss in this section unlawful restraint of an unwilling party, which is known as false imprisonment.

These matters are of more than academic interest. There is some possibility that a bellman or a waiter may lose his temper and strike a patron. A greater possibility is that a drunken patron of the inn, restaurant, or bar may become aggressive and threaten to strike, or actually strike, another guest. Under these circumstances, the management may have no alternative but to use physical force to eject the belligerent drunk, which could amount to assault and battery if carried out improperly. Another situation that might arise is one in which management must decide whether to challenge a patron who is suspected of stealing inn or restaurant property. This challenge could, if carried out improperly, result in a false imprisonment case.

Intent

Assault, battery, and false imprisonment all require intent on the part of the perpetrator. Essentially, intent is a common-sense term, meaning that the party wished to bring about a certain end. Thus, in battery the party wished to and did strike, hit, shoot, or otherwise impose an unwanted contact upon the victim. In assault, the party purposely offered or attempted to bring about a battery. In false imprisonment the party deliberately restrained the victim.

Assault and Battery

Assault and battery are usually considered together because they frequently occur together. A battery is simply an intentional, unpermitted contact,[1] and an assault is the offer or threat to commit a battery. Almost every battery involves an assault, because merely raising a fist or shaking a cane at a person will be considered an assault if that person is reasonably put in fear of being struck. Similarly, threatening to throw an object or pointing a gun would constitute assault; carrying out such acts to their conclusion would constitute battery.

Liability in assault and battery will be a danger to the hospitality operation any time that an employee threatens to, or actually does, strike a patron. This rarely happens, but good management practice requires that some care be taken to screen out employees who might have some history of violence or antisocial conduct.

It is true that in most states the employer is not held liable for intentional torts of the employee unless the act was closely connected with the employee's job, was authorized by the employer, or was ratified (approved) by the employer. Using these tests, in a case in which a bellman commits assault and battery on a guest who tipped him a nickel, the inn would probably not be held liable in an assault and battery case.

However, there are two problems in the above example. First, many states are increasing employers' liability for their employees' torts, and are asking merely, "was the tort related in some way to the job?" This could be found in the above example. Second, often the employer can be held for negli-

---

1. The contact need not result in actual injury, but might be merely offensive or insulting such as spitting on or slapping the plaintiff.

gence (which is considered in a later chapter) because he hired a potentially violent employee and should have known better. Thus, it is very important for any hospitality operation to screen out such applicants.

Another problem is that of the belligerent person in a bar. A bar has the responsibility of regulating conduct on its premises. The bar is not an insurer of its patrons' safety, but it is held to the standard of "reasonable care," which means that when a customer acts as if he might commit battery, the bar has the responsibility of seeing to it that he does not. This presents a dilemma for the bar. On the one hand, if a belligerent party is allowed to remain on the premises, the firm may well be liable for negligence if the rowdy customer subsequently assaults and batters another customer. On the other hand, there is always danger of a lawsuit in physically ejecting such a party, and the task of doing so should not be undertaken lightly. How is this dilemma to be resolved?

At the outset, it should be stated that there is a right to use reasonable force to eject unwanted parties from private premises, which would include bars located in hotels or restaurants. This right allows use of reasonable force under the circumstances, but does not include deadly force (threat to life or serious injury) unless the party involved seems intent upon committing murder or some other grave felony. What is reasonable force is very much concerned with what is necessary in a particular case.

Force that is absolutely necessary to eject someone creating a disturbance would almost always be considered to be reasonable. However, if merely asking a party to leave would seem to a jury to have been all that would have been necessary, any force beyond that would constitute assault and battery by management. As was said at the outset, ejecting patrons is a touchy process, and about the only advice to be given is: (1) do not use any more force than is needed, (2) use force only when necessary.

Discrimination in Ejection of Patrons

In formulating a decision as to whether or not to eject a person, or even to exclude him from entering an inn or restaurant, remember that hotels and motels are generally required to accommodate all well-behaved guests. Restaurants normally are not held to this requirement; private clubs, of course, may restrict the use of their facilities to members or guests, though in some states racial or religious discrimination could result in the loss of the club's liquor license. Hotels, motels, and restaurants are forbidden from discriminating on the basis of race, color, religion, or national origin, according to federal law and the law of many states. However, this does not mean that an individual is being discriminated against if he is ejected or excluded for unruly behavior.

False Imprisonment

False imprisonment consists of any unlawful restraint. A person need not actually be imprisoned; merely being ordered to remain in one place through threat of some dire consequence is sufficient to constitute false imprisonment. Therefore, it is dangerous to restrain persons suspected of shoplifting, of leaving without paying their bills, of crashing a private party, or even of damaging the premises.[1]

Let us consider the following situation. A guest had stayed at the inn for several days, and when he checked out, presented a personal check. A call to his bank was made, disclosing that his funds were insufficient to cover the check. This all happened while the guest was still waiting at the desk.

At this point, management is in a very delicate situation. On the one hand, the inn would like the bill settled or, at least, some further information about the guest and his solvency; but on the other hand, the danger of committing false arrest is obvious. In this situation, management should first point out that presenting a "non-sufficient funds" check is, in most states, a fraud against the innkeeper. Then management could ask the guest to voluntarily accompany the manager to the credit office to make other arrangements for payment. All of this discussion should be conducted in a quiet and friendly tone, without attracting the attention of other guests, in order to avoid a charge of defamation. If the

---

1. An important distinction should be made in this context. There is never a right to detain parties merely for nonpayment of debts. There is a right to detain parties who have engaged in criminal activity in the presence of the arresting party. Some states confine this right to cases where there is a breach of the peace. However, even in the latter case, the risks are considerable. If one makes a citizen's arrest of a guilty party, and if, for any reason (for example, confused witnesses, insufficient evidence to persuade the jury of guilt) the defendant is found not guilty, he may well sue successfully for false arrest, even though, in fact, he was guilty. Consequently, it is doubtful if the risks attendant in making a citizen's arrest can be justified. A detailed discussion of handling credit will appear in chapter 9.

guest follows and agrees to discuss other arrangements for payment, the inn is in a fair position to collect. If he refuses to come to the credit office, there is little the inn can do without some danger of liability for false arrest. They can ask for further identification, but the guest can refuse. Calling the police is of little assistance because, by the time the officers arrive, the guest may have long since walked out of the hotel and vanished. It is true that management has the right to make a citizen's arrest and, if the accused person is subsequently convicted, cannot be successfully charged with false imprisonment or assault and battery. However, if for any reason the accused party cannot be proved to be guilty, even though he may be guilty, management may well be successfully sued. Often it is doubtful whether making a citizen's arrest is worth the risk. (Probably the best recourse is to call the police and hope that they can arrive in time.)

All of the preceding points are equally applicable in food-service operations.

A similar case resulted when a couple asked for a room and, as they had no reservation, were required to pay in advance, which they willingly did. This was on a Friday. By Monday the bill had grown to $700 through large room-service charges and tips. When management demanded payment, the male guest indicated that he had lost his wallet. It turned out that employment and credit information on the registration card was incorrect. But this was of little consequence, because they had not fraudulently obtained credit. An intent to defraud the innkeeper could not be proved, because they had paid in advance to the extent to which they had been asked. (Intent is in a person's mind.) The hotel positioned an employee outside the guest's door to avoid his skipping (which does not constitute false arrest, but would if the employee actually did restrain the guest) and by this action helped the couple to another "free" night. When the persons volunteered to go to the airport to get a loan, the hotel gave up and did not exercise the right to hold the luggage, which was of little value. If the hotel had forcibly restrained the pair, management could have been liable for assault, battery, false arrest, and even possibly defamation (if accusations were overheard by a third party).

We will refer to this case at the end of the chapter when we will suggest certain procedures to be used to avoid this type of situation.

Defamation

We will now consider lawsuits that might arise from injury to patrons' reputations. For example, the hotel clerk or the waiter at the restaurant might, for some reason, doubt that the wife of a patron really is his wife. Or, either an inn or a restaurant might believe that a patron is leaving the premises with merchandise belonging to the firm and might be overheard by others while making such an accusation. The front office might dispute a patron's identity when he attempts to cash a check, or doubt the validity of his credit card. If sufficiently crude, accusations of this type might be defamatory if heard by others. Obviously, the tort of defamation presents some dangers which need to be seriously considered by the management of hospitality operations.

The Role of the Tort of Defamation

Defamation is the form of legal action by which one may recover damage for injury to his reputation. Defamation is sometimes referred to as the twin tort, because it really constitutes two separate torts with minor differences between them. These are libel, which consists of written or other permanently recorded defamations, and slander, which consists of oral defamations.

The tort of defamation cannot be classified as either an intentional tort or a form of negligence. The essence of defamation is injury to reputation, and this injury may result either intentionally or negligently. Protection to the victim is afforded in either case.

What Affects Reputation?

The first requirement of defamation is simply that some statement be made which, according to normal community standards, would affect someone's reputation. Obviously, whether a statement has this effect is a matter of community standards and subject to some differences of opinion. The traditional formulation is that the statement must tend to expose one to hatred, ridicule, contempt, or ill feelings. At common law, certain types of statements were held to be defamations per se, that is, assumed automatically defamatory. These included charges that the subject was a criminal, that he suffered from a loathsome disease, that he was incompetent in his trade or profession, or that an unmarried female was unchaste. We do not suggest these as a definitive list of what is defamatory, but they may provide some insight as to the sort of thing that is clearly defamation. We repeat, anything which would substantially affect the reputation of another can be defamatory; beyond that, the issue is mainly a question of judgment.

Communication

Before any form of statement may be defamatory, it must be communicated to some third person. One third person is enough, though some defamations in recent years have been communicated over national television and reached audiences of millions. This would normally affect the level of damages. On the other hand, some defamations have affected persons particularly important to the party defamed, as for example his wife; under these circumstances significant defamation, leading, for example, to divorce, could also result in heavy damages.

In most cases, there is no real issue as to whether communication of the defamatory statement occurred or not. That matter is usually clear. One exception might relate to the question of inference and innuendo. It is not necessarily a defense to defamation that one did not come right out and state his defamatory remark in plain language. The question is, was the meaning transferred from one mind to another—the mind of the third person. In other words, if defamatory inference and innuendo is clear enough that the third person recipient would understand who and what is supposedly involved, the tort has probably occurred.

Truth of the Statement

If whatever statement is claimed to be defamatory can be shown to be true, this will constitute a complete defense to any legal action. However, the burden is upon the person issuing the statement to prove that the statement was true, not upon the victim of the injurious statement to show that it was false.

Privilege

Finally, there are a number of forms of privilege available in an action for defamation, which means that, even though all the requisites noted above are present, there are special instances when other considerations outweigh the right to reputation; when such considerations are present, no suit can succeed. For example, persons writing references are protected by a privilege; even if what they say is incorrect, if the writer is honest, though mistaken, he cannot be held in defamation. However, there are not many instances in which the hospitality firm would be likely to be involved in these exceptions. Therefore, we will not pursue the subject here.

CASE

NEWTON v. CANDACE (GEORGIA 1956)
94 SE 2d 739

George Lee Newton filed an action against Candace, Incorporated, for damages resulting from physical injuries. The petition alleged in substance: that the defendant owned and operated the Briarcliff Hotel in Atlanta; that on March 22, 1952, at approximately 5 o'clock in the morning, the plaintiff, who was then a registered guest at the hotel, approached the clerk's desk in the lobby of the hotel, and the defendant's employee, the night clerk, "then and there furiously, suddenly, with malice, and without any provocation whatsoever, commenced to strike your petitioner a great number of violent blows upon his head and divers other parts of his body with a blunt instrument", that the night clerk was employed by the defendant at this time and place and was working within the scope of his employment in the defendant's business, with the defendant's knowledge and consent; and that petitioner received several permanent injuries from which he suffers and will continue to suffer pain, dizzy spells, and double vision.

The defendant's answer denied the material allegations of the petition.

Upon the trial of the case the plaintiff testified in part: that upon reaching their room in the hotel he had an argument with his wife and she left the hotel at approximately 2 o'clock a.m. and went to the Biltmore Hotel; that he then asked his friend, Mr. Eckerle, to accompany him to an all-night drug store where they had some orange juice; that he had drunk only two or three small drinks during the night; that upon returning to his room it occurred to him that his wife might have some difficulty in cashing a check at the Biltmore Hotel; that he then returned to the lobby and approached the night clerk, W. H. McMullen, who was on duty at that time; that he asked Mr. McMullen to establish a $50 credit at the Biltmore Hotel for his wife; that McMullen told him that the hotel had no connection with the Biltmore Hotel and that the best thing for him to do was to go there himself; that he insisted that the credit could be made at the Biltmore and McMullen told him that the hotel did not render this service nor did he have authority to do so; that as he began to count out the money, McMullen went into a small room behind the desk and returned and commenced to hit him on the head with a blackjack.

McMullen testified in part: that the plaintiff insisted that he establish a credit at the Biltmore Hotel for his wife; that he told the plaintiff that the hotel did not have facilities to establish the credit he desired; that he suggested that the plaintiff should either call or go to the Biltmore, himself, to establish the credit; that the plaintiff cursed him and reached for him over the clerk's counter; and that he then hit plaintiff with a blackjack.

Other witnesses testified as to facts which we feel are unnecessary to relate.

Syllabus Opinion by the Court

Quillian, Judge

1. Like other masters, a hotel proprietor or innkeeper is liable for the torts of his servant committed in the performance of the duties the servant is employed to discharge and that could be reasonably expected of him in the prosecution of the proprietor's business.

2. It is the duty of an innkeeper not only to furnish his guest or patron with shelter and comforts but also to exercise ordinary care to protect him from danger. 28 Am. Jur., Innkeepers, 6 52.

3. Hotels customarily transact business with patrons through the medium of clerks. It is within the scope of a hotel clerk's employment, when representing the proprietor of the establishment, to courteously reply to polite requests of the patrons for accommodations of a lawful and moral nature irrespective of whether he or the hostelry is under any duty or can reasonably be expected to grant such requests.

4. Where, as in the instant case, there was a conflict in the evidence, but some evidence supporting the contention of the plaintiff patron, that, when he tendered the necessary money for the purpose and politely requested of the defendant hotel proprietor's clerk that he arrange credit for his wife at another hotel, the clerk without provocation committed a violent assault upon him, thereby personally injuring and humiliating him, it was error to grant a nonsuit on the assumption that the clerk when making the attack was not acting within the scope of his employment or in the prosecution of the hotel proprietor's business.

Judgment reversed.
FELTON, C.J., and NICHOLS, J., concur.

* *Needless to say, this inn would have been much better off never to have hired the employee involved here. The court did not find that plaintiff had been offensive, but even if he had, that fact would have been absolutely no excuse for the employee's blackjacking the plaintiff.*

As stated in the preceding text an important issue in this sort of case is whether or not the assault and battery was closely connected with activities of the employee's job. Without much discussion of the problem, this court held that the necessary close connection was present.

CASE

BEGGERLY v. WALKER (KANSAS 1964)
397 P 2d 395

Background: The facts as alleged by the plaintiff, Beggerly, were as follows. Plaintiff entered the Eagle's Lodge in Parsons, Kansas. West, an employee of the lodge, was operating a crap game. Plaintiff began playing craps and became involved in an argument with West.

Davis was tending bar and in charge of the premises while Walker was assisting Davis in these duties. Plaintiff's wife asked Davis to call the police or to stop the quarrel himself, or she would call the police. Davis said he would stop the quarrel. He did not, but plaintiff's wife led plaintiff from the crap table. As he was proceeding toward an exit, Walker, without provocation, hit plaintiff and seriously injured him.

The trial court held that even if the facts alleged could be proved by plaintiff, there was no legal basis for holding Davis, West, or the Eagle's Lodge. Plaintiff appeals that ruling. The opinion on appeal follows.

Fronton, Justice

[1.] (Deleted) Not relevant.

[2,3.] The most casual glance at the petition will reveal a cause of action stated against Walker for assault and battery. Furthermore, when the petition is considered in its entirety, we believe it shows that plaintiff has framed his case against Eagles on the theory of *respondeat superior.*

[4,5.] We recognize the general rule, followed in Kansas as well as in other jurisdictions, that a master is not liable for a tortious act committed by his servant, including an assault and battery upon a third person, unless the act be done by authority of the master, either express or implied, or unless the act be done by the servant in the course or within the scope of his employment. Notwithstanding this rule, we believe that the facts set out in plaintiff's petition bring the case within an exception thereto, which, in brief, may be stated thus: That where an employee's duties involve the preservation of peace and order on the master's premises, or the protection of the master's property from loss or vandalism, an inference arises that the servant is expected to use reasonable force in the performance of his duties and, consequently, the use of force falls within the scope of the servant's employment.

The foregoing rule was recognized by this court in Lehnen v. E. J. Hines & Co., where an action was brought by a hotel guest for damages suffered from an assault upon her by the room clerk, among whose duties was the preservation of order. In this case, it was held:

"A hotel keeper is responsible to a guest for the acts of his servants in charge of a hotel, whether the particular acts were expressly authorized or not, providing the servant was acting in behalf of the proprietor at the time, and within the general scope of his employment."

In the course of its opinion, the court said:

". . . They placed him in authority as to the assignment

and occupancy of the rooms, and as to maintenance of order by the guests in the rooms; and they cannot escape liability where, in exercising his authority, he may have deviated from instructions, and because of a loss of temper or lack of sense and discretion he inflicted an unjustifiable injury upon a guest."

A comprehensive annotation on the subject is found in 34 A.L.R. 2d 412 et seq., where cases from numerous jurisdictions are collected in which recovery has been allowed against the operators of places of public accommodation, such as hotels, restaurants, bars and saloons, for injuries which their employees had inflicted on patrons of such establishments. From the allegations of the instant petition, the drinking and gambling club rooms open to the public or to guests which were maintained by the Eagles would clearly appear to be comparable to the businesses noted above.

[6.] Although the petition now before us alleges that the assault was made by Walker after the plaintiff's quarrel with West was concluded, it may reasonably be inferred from the circumstances that it was perpetrated in the course of Walker's employment to maintain order, even though unjustifiable force may have been used. The language of the petition is susceptible to the interpretation that Walker entered the room with Davis, who had primary charge of the club rooms, to assist Davis in putting an end to an argument between plaintiff and West which Davis had promised the plaintiff's wife he would stop; and that the blow was struck, either to end an argument which Walker and Davis did not realize was terminated, or to prevent further trouble from a quarrelsome guest.

[7.] Although it is not specifically so stated, it may also reasonably be deduced from the pleaded facts that Davis, after promising to end the disturbance, had enlisted Walker's help for that purpose and that the two men, both of whom were charged with preserving decorum in the club rooms, together approached plaintiff with such a purpose in view. Accordingly, it is our judgment that a cause of action is alleged against Davis, as well as against the Eagles. A different situation obtains as to West, whose only culpable conduct appears to have been his operation of a gaming table. No fact is alleged which infers that he had any responsibility to quell disorders or that he assumed to act in the capacity of a bouncer. We are constrained to conclude that his demurrer was correctly sustained.

[8.] What we have heretofore said disposes of the contention that no act on the part of Eagles or Davis is alleged to have been a proximate cause of plaintiff's injuries. If Eagles, on the principle of *respondeat superior,* and Davis, as an associate of or a participant with Walker in the actual assault, are liable for the injuries proximately resulting from the assault, then proximate cause, in the eyes of the law, will be attributed to both of them, in joint measure with Walker.

The judgment of the court below is sustained as to the defendant Earl West. The judgment is reversed as to defendants Bill Davis and Parsons Aerie No. 411, Subordinate Lodge of the Fraternal Order of the Eagles, with instructions that their demurrers be overruled.

It is so ordered.

✱ *This case, of course, will have to go back to the trial court for an actual determination as to whether the facts are as stated by plaintiff. However, the appellate court decided here that the plaintiff's claim makes out a case against Walker for obvious reasons (he perpetrated the assault and battery); against Davis, because, as the person in charge, he was responsible for maintaining order and for restraining Walker, and against the Eagle's Lodge because it was the employer. West really did nothing except get into an argument with plaintiff, and the court held that even accepting (for purposes of argument) the claim of plaintiff, there was no case against West.*

The key question again is, to what extent were the employee's actions related to his job? (The legal expression is "within the scope of employment.") The court here found legal authority for the proposition that where the preservation of peace and order is one of the employee's duties, assault and battery will normally be the employer's responsibility. In addition, this was specifically found to be one of the duties of employees who are hotel keepers.

CASE

CICUREL v. MOLLETT (NEW YORK 1956)
149 NYS 2d 397

PER CURIAM.

[1,2.] In this nonjury trial, the plaintiff sought recovery against the defendant upon two causes of action. The first charged that the defendant falsely caused the arrest of the plaintiff. After a trial the court below directed the entry of judgment for the defendant.

[3.] . . . In his answer the defendant alleged "the defendant caused the arrest of the plaintiff." While such an allegation in the answer is not conclusive, it may be accepted as an admission against interest and may be considered with the other proof in the case.

[4.] It was substantially established on the trial that the plaintiff was taken into custody in his hotel room by two police officers and detained there for a period of approximately eight hours. During that time the officers had numerous conversations with the attorney then representing the defendant. Moreover, in an examination before trial, portions of which were read into the record, the defendant admitted that he had been advised by the detectives that his attorney had instructed them to arrest the plaintiff sometime before the plaintiff was taken into custody. In sum, from all of the foregoing and the other proof adduced upon the trial, the inference is inescapable that the defendant caused the arrest of the plaintiff.

[5,6.] The arrest having thus been established, there is a presumption that it was unlawful and it therefore became incumbent upon the defendant to go forward with proof establishing justification. From the record we find that the defendant failed to establish justification for the arrest. We find upon all the proof and upon the inferences which fairly flow from the evidence that the plaintiff established his false arrest by the defendant.

[7.] As heretofore indicated, the plaintiff was detained in his hotel room by the detectives for about eight hours. Thereafter, he was removed to the station house, fingerprinted and booked, confined to a cell, and subsequently was arraigned in the Magistrate's Court charged with the crime of grand larceny. After several adjournments a hearing was held and the plaintiff was discharged. He was required to furnish bail in order to obtain his release after the first arraignment and was required to obtain counsel.

In the light of all the circumstances, we assess damages in the sum of $3,000.

All concur.

✳ *One is not liable for suit in false imprisonment or false arrest when he sincerely believes someone is guilty of a crime, has good reason to believe this, and reports the matter to police. This remains true even if the subject of the report should be indicted, tried, and found not guilty through some fortuity.*

However, that is not what occurred in this case. Evidently, the hotel persuaded the police to keep plaintiff captive in his hotel room for eight hours, without going through the procedures of informing him of the charges against him, informing him of his right to counsel and of his right to remain silent, and taking him before a magistrate, who could set bail.

Had defendant simply called the police, he would not have been liable, but having persuaded them to hold plaintiff illegally, defendant is liable.

CASE

MILLER v. STATON (WASHINGTON 1964)

FINLEY, J.

This is a personal injury action. It is now before this court on appeal for the second time. The facts and circumstances leading up to the injuries of the plaintiff-appellant Mary Miller are fully set out in *Miller v. Staton* (1961), 58 Wn. (2d) 879, 365 P. (2d) 333. Consequently, a brief summary of the facts will suffice as prologue to a consideration of the assignments of error which seem meritorious to us in the present appeal.

On New Year's Eve of 1957, the plaintiff and her husband, in common practice with many other Americans, were engaged in greeting the New Year at a party in a place of public accommodation, the "Pastime" Tavern, owned and operated by the defendants-respondents, at Omak, Washington. This particular New Year's Eve tavern party was open to the public. Obviously, it was not being held in a relatively swank and allegedly exclusive urban social club, but in a relatively popular social or gathering place in the expansive panoramic Okanogan country. The party, itself, was describable as crowded and exuberant—in fact, somewhat affected by the stock in trade offered for sale to the public by the *licensed premises.* The plaintiff was seated at a table with her back to the dance floor. About 2:20 a.m., a fight broke out between two gentlemen patrons of the establishment, who, after scuffling across the barroom dance floor, albeit somewhat unrhythmically, lurched into the plaintiff's chair, and quite unsociably to say the least, knocked her to the floor. The two gentlemen patrons of the establishment continued to fight above, over, and around her somewhat prone form on the tavern floor. Plaintiff was kicked and stepped on during the process, and the serious injuries she sustained as a result of the fracas are the subject of the present lawsuit.

The plaintiff's claim and this action for damages are based upon (1) the alleged negligence of the defendants in failing to provide proper police protection sufficient to maintain order and preserve the peace, and (2) the acts of an employee of the defendant (a waiter), who stood by watching the fight and made no effort to stop it before the plaintiff was injured.

The jury found for the defendants, and the plaintiffs appeal, setting out multiple assignments of error. Of these, mention need be made only of a few, as we find that the case must be reversed, and a new trial ordered.

3. Now, with the foregoing in mind, a third improper matter was put before the jury in the form of a contributory negligence instruction. In essence, this instruction indicated to the jury that it could legally find the plaintiff guilty of negligence simply because of her presence in the tavern at a time when it was crowded with loudly celebrating people who had been drinking. Such is not the law. The instruction conflicts with the disposition of the previous appeal between these parties (*Miller v. Staton, supra),* and unduly limits the scope of the established duty of the tavern operator toward the safety of his patrons. In order to justify the instruction, it would be necessary to find evidence of more

plausible acts of negligence on the part of the plaintiff beyond merely being present in the tavern. As there was no evidence introduced upon which a jury could base a finding in this regard, it was error to so instruct them. *Jablinsky v. Continental Pac. Lines, Inc.* (1961), 58 Wn. (2d) 702, 364 P. (2d) 793.

4. As further trial is necessary, one further assignment should be considered. The trial court excluded proffered evidence of an ordinance of the city of Omak which makes unlawful the selling of liquor after 1 a.m. Although the apparent violation of the ordinance present in this case would not amount to negligence per se, the jury is entitled to consider it in reaching its conclusions as to negligence and its disposition of the question of liability in this appeal.

On the basis of the above, the judgment is reversed, and a new trial is granted.

OTT, C.J., DONWORTH, WEAVER, and HAMILTON, J. J., concur.

* *Although suit in negligence was brought here, this case illustrates the fact that assault and battery of another patron may lead to suit against the host if he or his employees do not take reasonable steps to curb the violence.*

The action of the waiter in watching the fight without attempting to break it up could, when the case is retried, result in a finding of negligence on the part of the tavern.

Merely being present on New Year's Eve in a tavern is not contributory negligence. Consequently, the trial judge was in error, and the case will be retried.

Management Ideas: Intentional Torts and Defamation

1. When screening applications for employment, check to see if there is any history of fighting or other violence. Former employers will most likely cooperate.

2. Observe employees who are in contact with guests to see if they are unduly aggressive or antisocial toward guests or their own co-workers.

3. Train your employees to be alert to customers becoming belligerent toward other customers. Management has the duty to take precautionary steps in the event that this happens.

4. Instruct employees to call the supervisor when a chance of disturbance exists.

5. The supervisor should then very politely ask the guest to

leave, making sure not to threaten or touch him. A belligerent guest should not be given a second chance to remain on the premises, as illustrated in a case in which a patron attacked another patron and the injured patron held the owner liable for negligence.

6. If the guest will not leave, call someone on the premises if possible, such as another supervisor, the front office manager, or security guard, if available. Sometimes a show of determination will help.

7. As a last resort, escort the guest out, using as little force as possible.

8. It is perfectly legal to call the police, but what hospitality operation wants to call the police unless it is absolutely necessary?

9. Because of the possibility of suit for defamation, the above should go on very quietly, at least on management's side, and without accusations which could be overheard by a third party.

As far as false arrest is concerned, management should avoid a situation like the one described previously,* which resulted in the possibility of a suit for defamation. Here are some points as to how the "pre-payment situation" could have been avoided:

a. Ask for one night payment of any walk-in (person without reservation) who is not known to any management or front office personnel. Do not depend on the content of the luggage for security.

b. Mark guest's folio with a big red letter or sign indicating "walk-in."

c. Notify sales stations, such as dining rooms, room service, bars, switchboard, and recreational facilities of all walk-ins. Instruct the employees to require cash payment.

d. Instruct the front office staff not to post any charges on the folio of the walk-in guest but to return the oversight immediately to the department in which the oversight occurred. (This is possible only if the front office keeps up with posting charges.)

e. Alert the night auditor not to permit any charges.

f. In the morning at a reasonable time, inquire whether or not the guest wants to stay, at which time he should be required to again make an advance payment.

g. Set a limit on any guest account.

*See p. 37.

CHAPTER 4

Liability of the Hospitality Operation for Negligence

Introduction

IN THE PREVIOUS chapter, we discussed some instances in which a hospitality operation might be held liable for assault and battery, false imprisonment, or defamation. These torts usually involve a certain amount of human interest and make interesting reading. Moreover, they present a particular problem in that, to a large extent, insurers refuse to cover losses engendered in these instances.

Nonetheless, in terms of sheer frequency, the torts discussed in the previous chapter can hardly compare to the tort of negligence. Negligence is the source of more civil (i.e., non-criminal) litigation in our courts of record than any cause with the exception of divorce. Obviously, the manager of the hospitality operation must consider this problem in formulating his everyday plans.

Elements of the Tort of Negligence

A brief statement of the requirements of the tort of negligence is not very helpful in promoting an understanding of what is involved. However, we will begin with such a statement in order to give the overall picture and will then consider each of the requirements in detail.

To prove a case in negligence the plaintiff must show that the defendant was under some duty, that the defendant violated that duty, and that violation of a duty was the proximate cause of plaintiff's injury. Briefly, these requirements are: (1) duty, (2) breach of duty, (3) proximate cause, and (4) injury.

Duty

Ordinarily there is a duty to avoid injuring others. For example, if you carelessly drive your automobile into another car proceeding in the opposite direction or if you carelessly knock a glass off a window sill and it strikes a passerby, you are not adhering to your duty to avoid injuring others.

While ordinarily there is a duty to avoid injury to others, the duty is limited regarding some persons on private premises, including business premises. Hospitality operations owe a *general* duty to maintain reasonably safe premises for guests and other persons transacting business on the premises, but

TABLE 2

ROOM	NAME		RATE
SIGNATURE			ARRIVAL DATE
FIRM			DEPARTING
			NO. PERSONS / D. CLERK
ADDRESS			
CITY		STATE	ZIP
MAKE OF CAR		LICENSE NO.	STATE

GUEST REGISTRATION

NOTICE TO GUESTS: MANAGEMENT WILL NOT BE RESPONSIBLE FOR ACCIDENTS OR INJURY TO GUESTS. OR FOR LOSS OF MONEY. JEWELRY OR VALUABLES OF ANY KIND BY FIRE OR THEFT.

The notice on the above registration card, dealing with accidents and injury to guests, is meaningless since management cannot waive future liability for accidents or injury.

the duty is almost non-existent in the case of certain unin-
vited parties. For example, even though one leaves roller
skates on the stairs, if a burglar happens to suffer a broken
leg as a result, there is no duty owed the burglar.

Whether one owes a duty to persons entering his premises
depends upon why those persons are there. This question
may seem rather technical, but it is of great importance to a
hospitality operation because most injury cases will occur on
the operation's property.

Persons entering without permission, and contrary to the
wishes of management, are termed trespassers. The burglar
described above was a trespasser. In general, there is no duty
owed to a trespasser, aside from not deliberately injuring him
or not setting traps such as spring guns to snare him.

Persons may often enter hospitality operations with permission, but without intending to transact business. This situation might include solicitors for a worthy cause who had
been granted leave to enter, such as an outsider collecting
funds for the United Fund, a woman selling flowers in a bar,
and the traditional newspaper seller; also, persons waiting for
others, not guests, in the inn's lobby, restaurant, or bar, or
someone granted permission to use the restroom facilities or
the swimming pool. As to these parties, who are termed licensees, there is no duty owed to maintain reasonably safe
premises, but there *is* a duty to warn them of known defects.
For example, the manager of the restaurant granting permission to use the restroom might state, "Watch for the steps—
they are just being repaired." Or, "Go ahead, use the swimming pool, but be careful, the guard is not on duty."

Finally, those who are on business premises because they
are, or may wish, to conduct business are business invitees.
Guests in an inn and their invited friends and acquaintances,
patrons in a foodservice operation, and members of clubs and
their guests are the most obvious examples of invitees. But,
even parties entering the restaurant or lobby of a hotel to
buy a newspaper or some candy, or to shop in one of the stores
in a hotel are considered business invitees. To them there is a
duty to provide reasonably safe premises. That there is a fine
line between an invitee and a licensee is illustrated by the following example. A woman tried to deliver a message to a registered guest of a hotel. However, the guest was not in, and
the woman decided to wait. She went first to the TV room
and later to the "movie room." Upon entering the darkened

room she overlooked a flight of stairs, fell, and later sued for personal injury. The court decided that she was not an invitee, even though visiting a guest. It stated that she had overstepped the bounds of the invitation and had become, at most, a licensee.

Some states have broadened the definition of invitees beyond those conducting business, and in such cases the test is usually whether or not there was a "reasonable expectation" that safe premises would be provided. This test is rather difficult to delineate, but clearly, under this test, many parties who would otherwise be considered licensees may be considered invitees.

The duty to invitees is to provide reasonably safe premises. Even this does not make the hospitality operation an insurer of the guests' safety. Liability must be founded not only upon existence of a duty but upon breach of that duty through commission of a careless act, proximate cause, and injury.

Two points should be made in this context. First, from the perspective of planning, the above discussion is somewhat irrelevant, because generally the manager has no way of knowing whether a party who is destined to be injured may happen to be a trespasser, a licensee, or an invitee. If a dangerous condition exists, and the party injured happens to be a trespasser, this is simply a matter of relative good luck and not good planning on the part of the manager. All the manager can do is to provide safe premises, so that *no one* will be injured. Second, while there is a duty to maintain reasonably safe premises, this does not mean that the hospitality operation is liable every time someone is injured on its premises. The firm is not an insurer of its invitees' safety, and they may fall down stairs or out of a window through their own fault. The duty of the hospitality operation is merely to provide reasonably safe, not infallibly safe, premises. Some cases and examples will be cited at a later point.

Breach of the Duty

In negligence cases, the duty, if there is one, is breached by lack of reasonable care under the circumstances. We will refer to this lack of care as careless conduct.[1] In the hospitality

---

1. Many discussions of this subject refer to this breach of duty as "negligence." We avoid that term because one is then left with the anomaly of discussing "negligence" as *one* of the requirements of the *tort* of negligence, which is at best confusing.

industry, this usually means permitting an unsafe condition on the premises.

Careless conduct is as varied as the ingenuity (or lack of it) of man.

Fundamentally, what constitutes conduct sufficiently careless to warrant recovery in a legal action is a question of community standards. The jury in the case is asked to decide: did the defendant act as a reasonably prudent man? Did the act or omission of the defendant create an unreasonable danger of injury to persons or property? The jury decides this as a matter of judgment based on its own experience and local standards.

Examples of some conditions, that might be held to constitute careless conduct, of special relevance to the hospitality industry, are: snow, ice, or debris on stairs or walkways; defective elevators or unguarded, open elevator shafts; insufficient light; contaminated food or beverages; failure to supervice rowdy guests; failure to screen employees in hiring so that a larcenous or violent person is employed; and, of course, carelessness in driving a motor vehicle.[1] Here are some specific cases. A guest was injured when he tried to raise himself out of the tub by using the porcelain handle, which broke in his hand. A child was playing in a hotel room. The window, which was raised, had a screen. The child climbed up to the window sill, leaned against the screen, which gave way, and the child fell out of the window. (While the innkeeper is not obligated to put up screens on windows, if he does so, he must install them in such a way that they are reasonably safe.)

A guest preferred to use the stairs rather than the elevator in going from the lobby to his room. In the darkened stairway the guest fell and injured himself. This was an unsafe condition and management lost the case. Concerning the subject of elevators, management is not absolved from its duty to

---

1. Automobiles, of course, are the leading source of negligence suits in the United States. Many concerns have more problems from this source than does the typical hospitality operation. Nonetheless, if automobiles are operated by a firm at all, the following sources of liability are present:
   a. An unfit driver may be authorized by the firm to drive.
   b. The vehicle may in some way be unsafe. For example, brakes may be defective or tires worn.
   c. The driver may simply fail to use ordinary caution. For example, he might speed, run a stop sign, pass on the wrong side, or otherwise fail to observe prudent driving practices.

provide safe elevators, even ,if it has a maintenance contract with a firm specializing in this type of work.

Revolving doors are another source of problems. The glass panel in a revolving door broke and was temporarily replaced by beaverboard. A guest entered the hotel as someone else attempted to leave. The guest was injured, and the hotel was held to be at fault because an unsafe condition was present and was tolerated.

Swimming pools are often a source of problems.[1] For example, management tolerates "horseplay," or there is broken glass on the patio, or cleaning equipment near the pool—which in one case ended up in the pool where a guest was injured.

To avoid injury from broken glass, many operations have switched to plastic glasses and plates. There is understandably a resistance on the part of some hospitality operations to make this change. Plastic ware diminishes the esthetic value of food and beverages.

In some states, any violation of statute or state administrative regulation is considered negligence per se (that is, negligence in and of itself), in which case a finding of careless conduct is automatic. For this reason, if no other, it is important that there be no violation of fire, safety, or health codes. The lack of the use of a fire retardant material, blocking of exits, failure to provide rails, or insufficient refrigeration are just a few examples of conditions that may constitute a violation. Management will do well to ask for voluntary, periodic inspections by fire department and health department inspectors or to make arrangements for inspections with consultants.[2]

Proximate Cause

The mere fact that a careless act occurs does not mean that the perpetrator is liable for the tort of negligence. The careless act must be the proximate cause of an injury before liability will ensue. "Proximate cause" means essentially that

---

1. However, in virtually all, if not all, states, the mere fact of a guest drowning in a swimming pool is not proof of negligence on the part of the inn. Liability based on a drowning is established only when in some way a negligent act on the part of the inn is established. Not having a lifeguard on duty has uniformly been held *not* to constitute a negligent act.

2. For example, you can request a courtesy visit by an inspector of the Division of Labor and Industry under the Washington Industrial Safety and Health Act in that state (this is not possible under the federal Occupational Safety and Health Act).

there is a cause and effect relationship between the careless act and the injury. But it is more than this, because the word "proximate" means "immediate" or "direct." Normally the cause-effect relationship is obvious. In rare cases it may be so tenuous or unpredictable that the judge or jury is unwilling to call the careless act "proximate" cause of the injury and the case is held for the defendant.

Injury

Injury may be either to property, as when an automobile fender is dented or a building is damaged by fire, or to the person. Personal injuries tend to be the more expensive in terms of court judgments, partly because of the high cost of medical and hospital care; partly because, in a serious injury, there may be temporary or even permanent loss of wages as part of the judgment, and partly because an award for pain and suffering may also be included as part of the judgment. Often this portion of the judgment is several times greater than all the other portions involved in damage. For these reasons, the hospitality industry is probably more concerned with personal injury than with other forms of negligence suits.

Any personal injury may be the basis for a suit in damages (given the other requirements enumerated above). Usually, to constitute personal injury there must be some impact such as a fall, bump, shove, or collision. We have already cited a number of cases which resulted in personal injury. They involve more often than not defective windows; slippery or defective pathways and passages; glass doors, inadequate lighting, swinging and revolving doors; stairways and ramps; slippery or defective bathrooms, bathtubs, and showers; defective ceilings; defective furniture or equipment; defective elevators, and swimming pools. Here are some cases where injury was sustained but where no judgment against the hospitality operation ensued because no negligence could be shown. A boy fell from the top of a bunk bed. The parents claimed the boy fell because there was no rail. But the danger of falling ought to have been obvious to the plaintiff. An overweight man sat down on a luggage rack which collapsed. "Luggage racks are not for sitting," was the judge's comment. A mother carried her baby from the restaurant to a car in the parking lot. She tripped over a parking block and dropped the baby. The obstruction was obvious to anyone in the area. An older woman sitting at the edge of a dance floor in a restaurant was injured when she was accidentally hit by a pair of dancers. Because the dance floor was not crowded at the time, management had no obligation or duty to stop the dancers and, therefore, was not guilty of careless conduct.

Resume

Negligence is the most common form of law suit in the United States, excepting only divorce. However, it is important to remember that even though there is liability for injuries resulting from careless acts, a hospitality firm or other party is *not* an insurer against *all* accidents on the premises. An insurer is liable for injury regardless of cause. But a hospitality operation is not liable in negligence merely because an injury occurs. Before liability can be found, some careless act or omission must be found on the part of the person or firm being charged, and this must be the proximate cause of an injury. Otherwise, the injury in question is simply an unfortunate accident for which no one is liable.

Defenses

In all states, careless conduct by the injured party, which to some extent is a cause of his injury or aggravates his injury, will diminish his right to recover. Many states continue to adhere to the traditional rule of contributory negligence, which means that if the injured party's negligence was a proximate cause of his injury, even though the defendant was more negligent, no recovery will be allowed.

Other states have adopted the rule of comparative negligence, which means that if the injured party was negligent, his recovery will be decreased by the proportion of the total negligence that was his. In other words, if the injured party was found to be 30 percent of the cause of his accident, the recovery that he would otherwise have received would be decreased 30 percent.[1]

Most states continue to recognize the defense of assumption of risk. This means that if an injured party voluntarily and knowingly exposed himself to a risk and was subsequently injured, he is barred from recovery because he, in effect, con-

---

1. About 50 percent of the states have adopted comparative negligence, and the trend is clearly in that direction.

sented to the danger. For example, a guest uses a 10-foot diving board and injures himself. He has knowingly assumed the risk of danger. This does not mean that he was contributorily negligent. But, the effect is the same; he cannot recover. Note that these were reasonably safe premises, even though a guest was injured on the high board. Had he been injured because of a *defective* board, the innkeeper probably would have been liable.

We do not go into much detail on the question of these defenses for the simple reason that there is not much that management can do to cause a plaintiff to be contributorily negligent, or to assume a dangerous risk. These defenses depend entirely upon the conduct of the plaintiff. After an injury, an attorney might argue one of these as a defense, but management can only focus its attention on eliminating the possibility of negligence suits in the first place by maintaining safe premises and training employees to exercise care.

The Attractive Nuisance Doctrine

The attractive nuisance doctrine is a rather narrow exception to the general rule that the firm owes no duty to the trespasser. The doctrine applies only to children. When some installation or object is dangerous and is of such a nature that it would be expected to attract children because of its novelty or potential recreational value, then the obligation is upon the operation to anticipate that children will be attracted to the danger. Therefore, the firm must take reasonable steps to prevent children from being injured.

Special Relationships: Lodger and Tenant

Normally, patrons of hotels and motels are designated as guests. Characteristic of the host-guest relationship is that the inn be willing to accept all reasonably behaved applicants, that the guests are ordinarily travelers, that the stay is for short duration, and that the understanding is that most necessary services will be provided by the hotel or motel. In one case these services were described as: (1) providing maid service, (2) furnishing and laundering of linens, and (3) provision and upkeep of furniture and fixtures.

Hotels and motels may harbor persons under legal relationships other than that of host-guest, however. A lodger differs from a guest mainly in that he is a relatively permanent patron and is staying under a longer term contractual arrangement, but nonetheless has most services provided him.

A tenant contracts expressly or impliedly to have actual control of his premises, i.e., he normally provides his own furniture, may decide to redecorate if he wishes, and has the right to exclude everyone, including the management, from the premises except for occasional inspections to ascertain that he is not damaging the property. In this category one finds owners of businesses, such as dress shops, travel agencies, newspaper stands, and drugstores, who lease space from the hotel or motel management.

Any of these parties, lodgers or tenants, would qualify as business invitees when using the common halls, stairs, elevators, and lobby of the hotel or motel. Hence, there is little difference between the legal hazards presented by harboring these special classes of patrons and the previously described liability to guests. One important difference, however, is in regard to responsibility for premises under the control of a tenant. The management has no responsibility for these premises except to maintain the basic structure itself, i.e., roof, walls, and floors. But the responsibility for other maintenance (wax, water on the floor, for example) is the tenant's concern.

On the other hand, a lodger could recover on the basis of injuries caused by dangerous defects in his room, because he has not reserved exclusive possession in himself.

Fire and Act of God

Regardless of whether a patron of a hospitality operation is a guest or holds one of the special relationships described above, management could be responsible for injury caused by fire, *if* the fire was the result of its own negligence. For example, if management was negligent in permitting the fire to start, in allowing the fire to spread, or in inhibiting escape because of inadequate control measures or inadequate escape facilities, management would be liable. However, if the fire was due to unknown cause or "an act of God," and all fire code provisions were met, management would not be liable. "Acts of God" are events beyond human control or anticipation such as fires of unknown origin or general conflagration of a wide area, flood, tornado, and earthquake. Naturally, there is no legal liability for these events.

For Whose Conduct Is the Hospitality Operation Liable?

A fundamental premise of American law is that the employer is liable for the acts of his employee, when the latter is acting within the scope of his authority. "Scope of authority" is an ephemeral concept in borderline cases, but essentially it means "when on the job." When the employee is promoting the interests of the employer and is subject to the direction of the employer (whether the latter is present or not and whether the employer actually is directing the employee or not), the employee is acting within the scope of his authority. Needless to say, the employee need not be on the inn's or restaurant's premises to be on the job (he could be delivering something or running an errand), nor need he be acting within normal business hours. There is no one test for determining when the employee is within the scope of authority, but "advancing the interests of the employer" is probably the best approximation.

The employer is liable for the negligent acts of his employees performed within the scope of their authority. Therefore, the waiter who carelessly dumps a tray on the diner, the janitor who leaves an elevator shaft unguarded or who leaves obstacles or debris on the hallway, or the maintenance personnel who let snow accumulate on walks or entry-ways—all expose management to legal liability in negligence. It is the obligation of management to see that these dangers are not present.

Hospitality operations may also be liable for the actions of guests and even of trespassers if management tolerates the latter. This obligation rests upon a duty to take reasonable steps to regulate the behavior of persons using the facilities. For example, management operating restaurants and bars has a duty to regulate the conduct of patrons; if one patron becomes obstreperous and ends up injuring another, the injured party has a good chance of showing that management was negligent in not restraining or ejecting his attacker. The only issue is whether or not management should have reasonably realized that the obstreperous patron was presenting a danger. For example, during a New Year's Eve party, a guest of a restaurant is injured by one of two persons involved in a brawl. The restaurant owner owes a duty to his guests to protect them from other guests. The same is true of unruly guests of a hotel. Hotels have been held negligent when objects thrown out of windows by guests landed on passers-by. The issue here is whether management had notice that the guests were engaging in anti-social behavior.

All hospitality operations have a problem of what to do if a patron suddenly becomes ill. Essentially, there is a duty to take reasonable steps to care for ill patrons, which means, in other words, that a physician should be called if the illness appears at all serious. Hotels have been held liable for ejecting guests, even for non-payment of rent, who were ill and unable to care for themselves.

A hospitality operation may be found liable for bites inflicted on one guest by another guest's dog. In most jurisdictions, liability depends upon a finding that the hospitality firm should have realized the dangerous propensities of the dog, but in some jurisdictions liability is absolute, i.e., there is in effect no defense for having harbored a dog that turned out to be vicious.

In Event of Death on the Hospitality Operation Premises[1]

Perhaps surprisingly, there is no set, prescribed procedure that is legally required by most states to be followed in the event of death on business premises. However, there are some measures that would be appreciated by the police and which might, therefore, be considered the duty of a good citizen, and there are some measures which ought to be undertaken to minimize the possibility of civil liability.

Death may occur in a public place through a variety of causes, two of the more common being from a heart attack or from choking on a piece of food. In such cases, even if the victim is dead beyond any question in the mind of the manager, a doctor or, if aid would be brought more quickly, an ambulance should be called. The manager could be wrong in his judgment that the victim is dead, and, even if he is not, it might be difficult to prove at a later date that the party was not still alive and could not have been saved with proper care. If there is any question at all that the party might have been saved had proper steps been taken, the manager is exposed to the possibility of a lawsuit. For these reasons, the only course is to call a doctor or an ambulance, whichever would bring aid more quickly.

1. While not strictly confined to the question of tort liability, the authors felt that this issue was related and should be logically included within this section.

In some instances, death may result from violence, as in the aftermath of a hold-up or a brawl between patrons in a tavern. When this is the case, the police greatly prefer that the body not be moved. Moving the body may impede investigation. While in the short run this is apt to be bad for business, this eventuality is not likely to occur frequently, and probably cooperation with the police constitutes the greater good under the circumstances.

CASE

KARNA, PLAINTIFF,
v.
BYRON REED SYNDICATE
United States District Court,
D. Nebraska.
April 18, 1974.
(Nebraska 1974) 374 F. Supp. 687

Author's Statement of Facts

Defendants maintained a set of glass doors just adjacent to the check-in desk. Plaintiff checked in. When leaving, he walked into the glass door and injured himself.

DENNEY, District Judge

. . . The plaintiff's nose was cut and injured, for which he was treated at a local hospital. Subsequent repair surgery was also required and plaintiff suffered some pain until the end of May, 1971. A permanent scar remains on plaintiff's nose. Plaintiff lost two days of work from the accident and contends that the humiliation of having to explain the circumstances of his injury caused him to lose a raise and his job. Plaintiff seeks recovery for these damages and for the future embarrassment that will result when people ask and he must explain how he injured his nose.

Plaintiff contends that the doors were negligently designed, maintained and installed by the defendants. Plaintiff contends the glass should have been heavier, so it would not have broken; that the desk was too close to the doors; and that a metal push-pull bar should have been placed across the door to warn persons of its presence.[1] The defendants deny any negligence and allege that the plaintiff was contributorily negligent which should bar his recovery.

[1-3] The duty of the owner and operator of premises under these circumstances is to exercise ordinary care to keep the premises safe for the invitee plaintiff's use . . . Moreover, the owner and operator must take reasonable precautions to protect the invitees from foreseeable dangers in arrangement and use of the premises. . . . The duty of the architect is to use the standard of care ordinarily exercised by members of that profession, taking into account the foreseeable use of the building and persons or property that might be injured thereby. . . .

At trial, the expert testimony showed that, as originally constructed, the door met all specifications of ordinance and of custom in the city. It was not proved that any thicker glass should have been used in the door itself. It was also not proven, for the use intended, that a push-pull bar extending across the door was necessary for safety. . . .

[5] . . . Although the evidence does not show any individual breaches of their duties, i.e., the glass was too thin or the push-pull bar should have been used, it is the Court's finding that the arrangement, the placing of the desk in such close proximity to the inner glass doors, in combination with these other omissions, did constitute negligence. It was foreseeable that persons would stop at the desk, then quickly turn and leave. As the court said in Jiffy Markets, Inc. v. Vogel, . . . a similar case, "The invisibility of transparent glass, by its very nature, is likely to deceive the most prudent person . . ." Having that invisibility so close to the desk, without markings of any sort on the doors was an invitation for injury.

[6] However, the Court's inquiry is not finished. This is not the *Jiffy Markets* case, because the plaintiff was not unfamiliar with the dangerous condition. Plaintiff had gone in and out of those inner doors on three consecutive days. The Court finds that plaintiff knew, or should have known, of the dangerous condition of the interior of the lobby and registration desk in relation to the inner doors. . . . As such, the Court finds plaintiff was guilty of contributory negli-

---

1. Plaintiff has also alleged breach of warranty, but the Court Can find no basis in law or fact for this claim.

gence in a degree more than slight in relation to the gross negligence of the defendants, Byron Reed Syndicate No. 4 and Byron Reed Company, Inc., to bar his recovery for his damages.

An order denying recovery and dismissing this case will be entered contemporaneously herewith.

* *The moral in this case should be clear to the inn. Although they won this case, because plaintiff was shown to have been familiar with the door in question, another time a plaintiff might be injured on his first passage through, or into, the door. The outcome of that suit might not be so fortunate for the inn.*

It is essential that management personnel be alert to dangers of this sort and take steps to correct them.

CASE

HULL
v.
HOLIDAY INNS OF AMERICA, INC.
v.
H. COMINS
Nos. 72-1549, 72-1550.
(Michigan 1973) 478 F. 2d 224

(Held for defendant at trial court.)

PER CURIAM

. . . The plaintiff brought an action against Holiday Inns of America, as defendant, to recover damages for injuries alleged to have been sustained by excessively hot water in the bathtub of a Holiday Inn in Detroit, Michigan. Holiday brought in other parties as third party defendants but this opinion will involve only the plaintiff and defendant as briefed by the parties.

The plaintiff had been a guest of the Inn in question for thirty-five days and on the morning of September 11, 1967 he undertook to take a bath in the bathtub. He turned on the hot water, only, and in attempting to test the temperature of the water while sitting on the edge of the tub, he slipped in the tub and sustained the injuries of which he complains. The plaintiff received severe burns on his right hand and right buttocks.

It is claimed on behalf of the plaintiff that the water in the bathtub was excessively hot, of a temperature in excess of what is regarded as safe for such use and that the defendant violated its duty to maintain its premises in a reasonably safe condition for plaintiff, as an invitee. The severity of plaintiff's injury is not in question. It was admitted for the purpose of the motion for a directed verdict that if the defendant supplied water in excess of 150°F.[1] to plaintiff's room for bath purposes it would have been in excess of that customarily permitted and regarded as safe.

The district judge in granting the motion for judgment of no cause of action held that the plaintiff had failed to offer evidence that the temperature of the water was in excess of 150°F. or that the defendant had violated its duty toward plaintiff to maintain its premises in a reasonably safe condition.

Obviously, there is no evidence available of the exact temperature of the water at the time the plaintiff fell into the tub and received his injuries. Mechanically, there was a separate boiler to furnish hot water to the rooms of the motel. The gauge on it was set at 180°F. There is a Holby Mixing Valve which mixes the hot water as it comes from the boiler with cold water to a proper temperature for the rooms. There is a gauge or thermometer on this Mixing Valve to regulate the temperature of the water that goes to the rooms. There is no evidence of the temperature at which that gauge or thermometer was set. There was also a limit switch which was supposed to cut off when the water got up to a certain temperature. There is no evidence of the temperature setting of it or whether it was functioning.

Dr. Joseph D. Carlysle, a plastic surgeon who treated the plaintiff, testified that the nature of plaintiff's burns were such as might be received in water of 180°F. in thirty seconds. He did not testify whether such burns could be received in water of a temperature of 150°F. or less or how long it would take to get such burns as the plaintiff had in water of 150°F. or less.

---

1. It was undisputed that a safe temperature of water for rooms in a motel or hotel was 140°F., plus or minus five or ten degrees.

The plaintiff testified that he turned on the hot water and sat on the side of the tub. When he reached over to test the water with his hand, he slipped and fell into the tub. He caught himself on his right hand and right hip and as he went down he bumped his head on something which caused a bump on his head as reported by the hospital. To extricate himself he reached for the basin, which was right by the tub, with his left hand and pushed himself out with his hand and hip. In the process he knocked a glass off of the basin which broke on the side of the tub and caused some cuts on the left hip and left buttocks.

He testified further that he was in a daze and didn't know exactly how long he was in the water. He said he got up as fast as he could and estimated that he was in the water seven, eight or ten seconds.

Dr. Carlysle testified,

"The infliction of a burn depends on the temperature of the agent, the duration that the patient is in contact with the agent, and also the area of the skin involved, and even the age of the patient." . . .

"To have these burns inflicted, the water would, in my opinion, have to be excessively hot—as I said before, in excess of 150, and even approaching ranges of 180 and above." On cross examination he testified that at 135°F. one might receive burns comparable to the ones the plaintiff had in five minutes.

[2] Thus, a crucial fact in the case is the length of time the plaintiff was in the water. We consider that the jury is entitled to draw inferences from the physical facts as well as the oral evidence. We conclude from the fact that only the plaintiff's right hand and right buttocks were burned the jury might well infer that no other part of his body was in the water and that he could not have remained in that position over a few seconds which would indicate that the water was excessively hot.

[3] Counsel for the defendant argues that the plaintiff was guilty of contributory negligence as a matter of law. The district judge did not decide this question. We consider, however, that it is a question for the jury to decide under all the facts of the case.

Judgment reversed and the case is remanded to the District Court for trial to a jury.

✱ *There is no complex legal issue to be decided here. The question is, simply: was the water which clearly burned plaintiff unreasonably hot? The appellate court held merely that a jury must decide the question.*

Clearly this case suggests something the prudent innkeeper should check. Just how hot is your water? Do you know for sure?

CASE

TARSHIS
v.
LAHAINA INVESTMENT CORPORATION
No. 71-2725.
United States Court of Appeals,
Ninth Circuit.
June 21, 1973.
(Hawaii 1973) 480 F. 2d 1019

PER CURIAM

This appeal is from a summary judgment of dismissal awarded to Lahaina Investment Corporation, d/b/a Royal Lahaina Hotel, on the ground that no genuine issue of material fact was involved.

[1] Appellant, a citizen of New York, registered with her husband at the Royal Lahaina Hotel at Kaanapali, Maui, on January 27, 1969. The Royal Lahaina with a beach frontage of 400 feet advertised in brochures that:

"[The] Royal Lahaina Beach resort stretches along a 3-mile secluded white sand beach on the West side of the Island of Maui. . . .The sea is safe and exhilarating for swimming . . ."

However, on the day of appellant's accident, appellee alleges that four signs were posted along the frontage of the beach, two of which read:

"CAUTION Red flag on beach indicates dangerous surf conditions. Guests please use swimming pools. Mahalo."[1]
The other two signs read:

"NOTICE to our guests, Red Flag on Beach indicates dangerous surf. Please use swimming pools. Mahalo."

---

1. Mahalo is an Hawaiian word, meaning "thank you."

The red flags (allegedly six in number) were positioned along the edge of Royal Lahaina's beach frontage, and were admittedly seen by appellant on January 28 when she, her husband and friends, went to the beach to swim in the ocean. Appellant, however, in her affidavit, stated that she did not see the signs of warning of dangerous surf conditions, nor did she receive verbal warnings from appellee concerning those conditions. Noting the existence of "slight waves," appellant and her companions entered the water where, five to ten minutes later, appellant was injured as the result of being thrown on the beach by a "huge wave."

[2] In granting appellee's motion for summary judgment the district court assumed, without deciding, that appellee owed appellant the duty to warn her of dangerous conditions in the Pacific Ocean along its beach frontage "which were not known to her or obvious to an ordinarily intelligent person and either were known or in the exercise of reasonable care ought to have been known to the [appellee]." We find this to be a correct statement of the law. . . .

[3] The court held, however, that the dangers inherent in swimming in the ocean on the day of the accident "should have been known to the [appellant] as an ordinarily intelligent person" and hence appellee was under no duty to warn appellant of the dangerous surf conditions.

Whether or not the ocean fronting appellee's property would have appeared dangerous to an ordinarily intelligent person is a question of fact inappropriate for summary adjudication. We have recently noted that " 'issues of negligence are ordinarily not susceptible of summary adjudication'." . . .

Appellant contends that she observed only "slight waves," and saw nothing to indicate the powerful force exerted by some of them. Appellee presented evidence that the surf on the day of the accident was "like that usually experienced during a typical trade wind day," but came forward with nothing to show that appellee should have known that the surf was dangerous as the hotel itself cautioned in its signs.

On the basis of this evidence, appellant is entitled to present to a trier of fact her theory that the existence of the powerful, surging surf represented an unapparent, dangerous condition which appellee knew about and of which it failed to adequately warn her.

The judgment is reversed and the cause remanded to the district court.

* *Summary judgment referred to in the first paragraph of this case consists in a trial court deciding a case merely on the basis of the statement submitted by the plaintiff and the defendant, but without hearing any witnesses or receiving any other evidence.*

A summary judgment is not proper when there is a question of fact to be decided, and here there was. The significant question was, did the hotel owe a duty to warn guests of the danger of swimming on the day plaintiff was injured? This will be up to a jury to decide, but the appellate court clearly holds there is a strong possibility that such a duty is present.

CASE

MONTES

v.

BETCHER D/B/A THE HAGEN RESORT
(South Dakota 1973) 480 F. 2d 1128

NICHOL, District Judge.

On the warm Sunday afternoon of July 13, 1968, 35 year old Fernando Montes, a citizen of Nebraska, took a running dive off a short dock which served the Appellant's resort, one of the many enhancing Minnesota's beautiful lakes. He surfaced with a severely lacerated scalp and a vertebral fracture. Shortly after the incident, a jagged piece of concrete was recovered from the lake floor in the general area where plaintiff had entered the water. The concrete piece resembled the homemade boat anchors constructed by Appellants to use in the boats which frequented the boat dock.

Plaintiff, Montes, a proficient swimmer and diver, claims that he executed a flat, "racing" dive because he knew he was plunging into shallow water. The water depth was variously described to be from 27 in. to waist level. Montes testified, however, that his ultimate purpose was to grab the ankles of a friend who was standing in the water 15 feet from the end of the dock, a purpose which would require either a deep dive or a subsequent submergence.

Montes was very familiar with the swimming area, and had executed dives from the boat dock on numerous previous occasions. Never before had he encountered rocks or blocks in the water. He admitted to having imbibed two or three drinks on the afternoon of the accident.

The Appellants, Mr. and Mrs. Betcher, citizens of Minnesota, had owned the resort since 1963. They charge $10 per day for cabin accommodations. Although the area surrounding the boat dock was perennially in use by Appellants' swimmer-patrons and although Mr. Betcher had seen swimmers jump off the boat dock, he testified that he had never made any special attempt to inspect the lake bottom for debris nor had he ever "raked" the shoreline lake bottom. Never had he erected signs warning of the dangers of diving in the shallow water or the possible presence of debris in the swimming area. Never had he placed floats in the water to discourage the intrusion of boats into the swimming and diving area; in fact there was no segregation whatsoever of swimming waters from boating waters.

The case went to the jury on a comparative negligence instruction. The jury adjudged defendants 90 percent negligent and the plaintiff 10 percent negligent. The Appellants-defendants challenge the sufficiency of the evidence to support submission to the jury and the Trial Court's refusal to instruct on assumption of risk.

[1] A jury must not be denied the right to make reasonable inferences from the evidence. . . .Given that premise, we conclude that the jury could have reasonably inferred that the Appellee came into contact with the concrete block rather than with the bottom of the lake.

Appellant's challenge to the submission of the case to the jury is based upon a contention that the Trial Court was mistaken in the formulation of Appellant's duty to their guests. They first contend that a riparian owner is not responsible for the safe maintenance of property beyond the meander line of a lake, which line marks the boundary between Appellant's shoreline land and submerged land which belongs to the state. But even if Appellants are held responsible for the maintenance of submerged lands, Appellants contend, that responsibility extends only to the remedy of dangerous conditions known to Appellants or of which they could have acquired knowledge had they been in the exercise of reasonable care. Since there was no evidence that Appellants knew of the presence of the cement block nor that it had been there long enough to mandate an invocation on constructive knowledge, Appellants contend the case should not have gone to the jury.

[2, 3] The Trial Court correctly rejected these formulations of duty (or lack thereof). Relying upon the case of Hanson v. Christensen, . . .the Court held a resort owner who avails himself of the advantages of riparian ownership for resort purposes owes to his patrons a duty of reasonable care which includes "active vigilance" in their protection from foreseeable risks. . . .The Court thus rejected the necessity of showing actual knowledge of the existence of the dangerous condition or of showing that the condition was of sufficient duration to afford constructive notice, which are the ordinary standards of care in the business invitee situation.

[4-6] The jury was perfectly justified in determining that Appellants had violated this duty in any one or more of three respects: (1) their failure to warn of the dangers of diving off the boat dock; (2) their failure to periodically "rake" the swimming-diving area in search of dangerous obstructions; (3) their failure to segregate swimming areas from boating areas. In the absence of any evidence of an intervening-superseding cause, the jury was also justified in concluding that the Appellant's omissions were the cause of Appellee's injuries. The jury's allocation of negligence between the Appellants and the Appellee pursuant to Minnesota's comparative negligence statute, . . .is determinative absent a showing that there was no evidence to support it. . . .That clearly is not the case.

[7, 8] Appellants also contend that the Trial Court's failure to instruct on assumption of risk warrants reversal and a new trial. Marshalled against this position are Appellee's arguments that, first, Appellants failed to submit a timely request for the instruction and, second, the merger of the defense of assumption of risk into the defense of contributory negligence, declared by the case of Springrose v. Willmore, . . .applies to abrogate the necessity of instructing on assumption of risk. We find it unnecessary to treat

these arguments because we cannot find sufficient evidence in the record to support an instruction on assumption of risk. To justify an instruction on assumption of risk, there must be evidence to support three jury findings: (1) that plaintiff had knowledge of the risk; (2) that he appreciated the risk; (3) that he had a choice to avoid the risk or chance it and voluntarily chose to chance it. ... The risk of which we speak is the risk of coming into contact with the cement block and not the risk of hitting the lake bottom. "The fact that the plaintiff is fully aware of one risk, as for example that of the speed at which a car is being driven, does not mean that he assumes another of which he is unaware, such as the failure of the driver to watch the road." ... There is no evidence in the record that Appellee was aware of, appreciated, or voluntarily assumed the risk of hitting the cement block. He had executed many dives from the boat dock and never had he encountered obstructions. One witness testified that it was the usual practice for experienced swimmers to dive off the boat dock and swim to the diving dock anchored off-shore. Appellee testified that he had been vacationing at the resort every summer since 1963 and never had he encountered stones or blocks in the water. Appellee could hardly have assumed a risk of which he was not aware.

We therefore find that there was sufficient evidence to support a plaintiff's verdict and that the defense of assumption of risk is inapplicable to this fact situation.

Affirmed.

＊ *No one claims that a resort owner must provide lake facilities, but probably the main income of the resort depended upon the lake. Here, again, the inn failed to adequately inspect its facilities or to take proper precautionary steps. The result was disaster.*

CASE

YOUNG
v.
CARIBBEAN ASSOCIATES, INC.
Civ. No. 395/1970.
District Court, Virgin Islands,
D. St. Thomas and St. John
April 23, 1973.
(Virgin Islands 1973) 358 F. Supp. 1220

MEMORANDUM OPINION

WARREN H. YOUNG, District Judge.

This is a tort and breach of warranty action tried by the Court without a jury. A father and his ten-year-old son seek recovery for mental anguish suffered by the father and bodily injuries suffered by the son brought about in unusual circumstances. The son, Francis Howard Young, was staying with his parents at the defendant Caribbean Beach Hotel. On New Year's Eve, 1969, the family was having dinner in the hotel dining room. At the end of the meal, the son volunteered to go through the dessert serving line to bring a Cherries Jubilee for his father. As the son reached the head of the serving line, the waiter in charge of flaming and serving the Cherries Jubilee found it necessary to kindle the flames by adding more rum to the chafing pan. He took a bottle of hundred-and-fifty-one proof rum, which was stoppered with a narrow "slow pour" spout, and proceeded to pour the rum directly into the pan. As he did so, the spout either dropped out or was popped out by an internal combustion in the rum bottle and a quantity of volatile rum gushed out. An abnormally high flame resulted, which reached out to touch the boy, setting his shirt on fire. The boy suffered severe burns and has undergone considerable treatment for skin and flesh grafts and plastic surgery. The several . . . clauses in the multiple counts of the amended complaint request $200,000 compensatory damages and $100,000 exemplary damages for the son and $19,912 medical specials and $25,000 mental anguish damages for the father. The complaint bottoms recovery principally upon negligence of all defendants, but the breach of warranty and products' liability allegations were aimed primarily at Sears, Roebuck & Company, the vendor of the allegedly highly flammable boy's shirt.

[3] The father's right to recover his expenditures for medical specials and the son's right to recover compensatory damages for his bodily injuries are clear. The hotel is, at the very least, accountable for its serving waiter's negligence in using an improperly stoppered bottle, which permitted the "slow pour" spout either to fall out or pop out, thereby discharging a large quantity of volatile rum. Moreover, as the evidence tended to show, the hotel's serving waiter was negligent in the first place in pouring the rum directly from the bottle and not from an intermediary bowl or pitcher. An experienced maitre d'hotel and chef testified that to pour directly from a bottle was to invite the flame to catch onto the stream of rum and leap from the chafing pan to ignite the vaporous gases inside the bottle, blowing out the cork and turning the bottle into a veritable "flame thrower" or "blowtorch," capable of throwing a flame ten or fifteen feet. Although I need not decide that this in fact did happen, I do find that it was negligent to pour directly from the bottle and not from an intervening bowl or wide mouth pitcher. In a sense, the dessert waiter does not seem morally culpable for he had not been trained in the proper handling of flambes. Nonetheless, he and his employer should be responsible for the injuries caused to the boy, no matter how inadvertently they came about.

[4] I further find that the negligence of the hotel and its serving waiter was the sole and proximate cause of plaintiff's injuries. The hotel for a time relied in part on the theory that the boy's shirt was itself highly flammable as evidenced by the vigor with which it burned and that this was an important intervening cause of the holocaust that developed. With this theory in mind, as well as the thought of allocation of damages between joint tort-feasors, the hotel impleaded Sears, Roebuck & Company as a third-party defendant. At the trial, however, a written statement of the waiter was produced which indicated that a substantial quantity of the rum had gushed directly onto the boy's shirt. This itself would be more than enough to support the combustion, no matter what the flammability of the shirt fabric might be. The third-party complaint against Sears was therefore dismissed upon the motion of plaintiff and Sears' counsel, with no objection raised by defendant's counsel. The action then proceeded against the serving

waiter and the hotel alone. I also find that the boy was not guilty of contributory negligence. Although there was some testimony indicating that he was warned to stand back, the warning would have been, at the very best, an insufficient caution to a normal boy of plaintiff's years.

(Note: The remainder of the lengthy opinion was devoted to the question of how damages that had already been decided were to be measured.)

Special precautions must be taken any time volatile materials are being handled. Rational, standardized procedures in the use of the flammable, together with proper training of the employee involved, could well have eliminated the possibility of this accident occurring.

CASE

STAHLIN
v.
HILTON HOTELS CORPORATION
(Illinois 1973) 484 F. 2d 580

ESCHBACH, District Judge.

This diversity action resulted in a jury verdict against defendants Andersen and Hilton and a directed verdict in favor of defendant Addenbrooke. The jury fixed damages in the amount of $150,000 in favor of Aloysius Stahlin and $60,000 in favor of his wife Louise on her loss of consortium claim. We affirm as to Andersen and Hilton.

The primary questions raised on appeal by Andersen and Hilton relate to the sufficiency of the evidence to support the verdict against them, the propriety of the trial court's action in relieving plaintiffs of a certain pre-trial stipulation, and the correctness of certain instructions given the jury.

Plaintiff Al Stahlin checked into the Conrad Hilton Hotel in Chicago, Illinois, on May 24, 1966, for the purpose of attending a sales convention. After an afternoon at the race track, he and Mr. Ken Bishop returned to their room at the hotel and began to get dressed for a company dinner that evening. As Stahlin was hurriedly dressing, he got his foot tangled in his shorts, fell backward and struck his head against the wall about two and a half feet above the floor. Stahlin had to be helped to his bed by Bishop, and the two men stayed in the room rather than attend the company dinner. Stahlin complained of a headache, and Bishop observed a bruise or blood coming to the surface at the back of Stahlin's head. A short time later that evening, Stahlin became nauseous and vomited. Bishop then decided to call the management of the hotel for a doctor. Bishop spoke to the assistant manager, described what had happened to Stahlin and was told that "some help" or a doctor would be sent. Fredarica Andersen came to the room about half an hour later and identified herself as a nurse. After learning the facts of the occurrence from Bishop, she examined and felt the back of Stahlin's head and took his temperature, blood pressure and pulse. She observed a bottle of pills on the table next to the bed and learned that Stahlin had a prior heart condition. Bishop testified that she and Stahlin discussed the fact that the pills were a blood thinner or anticoagulant he was taking for the heart condition. Stahlin complained to her of a terrific headache, and she further learned that he had vomited earlier. Before she left, Mrs. Andersen told Stahlin to stay in bed for twelve hours.

Mrs. Andersen died prior to trial. The following record which she made of her visit was received in evidence:

Pt was putting on his trousers and fell against the wall in his room, bumping back of head. Before this happened, he had been to the race track, had several drinks, ate a beef sandwich, and vomited contents of food and liquor. Pt took a codeine derivative tablet—also has a coronary condition, refused to go to hospital, will stay in bed for 12 hours. 13/p—15-5/8—tem.98.6 F.A.

Bishop testified that Mrs. Andersen said nothing to Stahlin about seeing a doctor or about going to a hospital. Stahlin did not testify.

Stahlin slept uneasily that night and was up several times. He vomited four or five times. Stahlin remained in the room the next morning when Bishop left to attend the 9 a.m. meeting of the convention. When he returned to the room between 12:00 and 12:30, he found Stahlin in a semi-comatose state. An ambulance was called and Stahlin was taken to the hospital. He was diagnosed as having a sub-dural hematoma. Surgery was immediately performed to relieve the pressure on plaintiff's brain caused by the large blood clot or hematoma. Plaintiff suffered residual brain damage.

In addition to the foregoing sequence of events, the evidence at trial established that Mrs. Andersen, although commonly referred to at the hotel as a nurse, was not in fact licensed in the State of Illinois either as a registered nurse or a licensed practical nurse. She had been employed for many years by Dr. Addenbrooke in the medical department of the hotel, which department was under his supervision during its entire period of existence from 1948 through 1968. For some time prior to and including the month of May, 1966, the medical department was without the services of a physician during the nighttime hours. Dr. Addenbrooke left Mrs. Andersen in charge of the medical department at night with the full knowledge and consent of the hotel management. During these hours it was the practice of the hotel to refer guests in need of medical assistance to Mrs. Andersen. She charged a standard rate of $15.00, the same amount charged for a doctor's night room call. This amount was added to the guest's bill, collected by the hotel, and remitted to Dr. Addenbrooke in accordance with their long-standing practice. Dr. Addenbrooke let Mrs. Andersen use her own judgment in making room calls and merely provided her with a list of specialists to whom she could refer guests. Mrs. Andersen did not consult with Dr. Addenbrooke concerning her room calls and her findings were not reviewed by him.

[1-3] We believe the evidence was sufficient to support a finding that Hilton was negligent in sending Fredarica Andersen to Stahlin's room in response to Bishop's request for help. Whether Bishop specifically requested a doctor and whether the assistant manager represented that a doctor would be sent are not determinative of this question. Bishop related the circumstances of Stahlin's problem and Hilton undertook to render assistance. As the trial court correctly charged the jury, "the operator of a hotel owes no duty to provide any service for a guest who may be ill or injured. If, however, it undertakes to provide such service for any person, it must exercise ordinary care to provide such services that it has undertaken to give." *See* Nelson v. Union Wire Rope, . . . We agree with plaintiffs that the duty

undertaken by Hilton was more than merely "sending someone up" to Stahlin's room. Reasonable care under the circumstances required that the hotel send a doctor, or at the
very least, a licensed nurse, to provide the medical assistance
requested on behalf of Stahlin. Moreover, while Hilton denies that it had knowledge of Mrs. Andersen's lack of a license, there is ample evidence in the record from which the
jury could find that the failure to inquire as to her qualifications constituted negligence on the part of Hilton. Hilton
knew she was making room calls on sick and injured guests
and charging the same amount as a doctor. It was the established practice of the hotel to send her to a guest's room in
response to a request for a doctor. Under these circumstances, since Hilton knew she was not a doctor, the jury
could reasonably find the hotel chargeable with such further knowledge which a reasonable investigation would have
revealed—that is, that Mrs. Andersen was not a licensed
nurse. Hilton replies on Tansey v. Robinson, . . . in support
of its position that plaintiffs were required to show that the
hotel had actual knowledge of Mrs. Andersen's lack of qualifications. However, the court in *Tansey, supra,* held that
liability for the negligent acts of an independent contractor
may be predicated upon a failure to exercise reasonable
care in selecting a careful and competent contractor. The
defendant there hired a truck driver who had a record of
29 convictions for traffic offenses, whose license had been
taken away from him, and who had no permit to carry
property for hire. Although the defendant contended that
it had no actual knowledge of the driver's incompetence
and had made reasonable inquiries, the court held that the
foregoing were "matters which could have been determined
by the A & P upon inquiry, and they are matters which a
trier of fact may take into consideration in determining
A & P's liability." . . .Hilton states in its brief that both
Dr. Addenbrooke and Mrs. Andersen were independent
contractors. Thus, under the rule stated in *Tansey, supra,*
Mrs. Andersen's lack of a nursing license in Illinois was a
matter which could have been determined by Hilton upon
inquiry, and it was a matter which the jury could properly
take into consideration in determining whether Hilton was
negligent in carrying out its voluntary undertaking to provide medical assistance for Stahlin. . . .

[9] Finally, we are persuaded by a review of the evidence as it relates to the alleged negligence of Dr. Addenbrooke in authorizing Mrs. Andersen to engage in extensive diagnosis and treatment activities that the trial court erred in directing a verdict in his favor. The evidence showed that Mrs. Andersen, although not even a licensed nurse, was permitted to make room calls on sick and injured hotel guests, and was permitted to use her own judgment without benefit of instructions from Addenbrooke other than a list of medical consultants, and without subsequent review of her findings by Addenbrooke. She charged the same amount for a room call as a doctor, which amount was collected by the Hilton and remitted to Addenbrooke. Thus, there was evidence in the record from which the jury could find that Addenbrooke permitted and authorized Mrs. Andersen, as a general practitioner and on the particular night in question, to perform duties performed under Illinois law only by licensed physicians. ...The acts performed by Mrs. Andersen with respect to Stahlin could reasonably be found to constitute medical diagnosis, prescription, and treatment so as to fall within the foregoing statutory prohibitions. Given this state of the record, the jury should have been permitted to consider whether the delegation of such duties by Addenbrooke to Mrs. Andersen constituted negligence and whether such negligence was a proximate cause of Stahlin's disability. ...

Accordingly, the judgment is affirmed as to the defendants Hilton and Andersen.

---

* *In the early portion of this case it was mentioned that the inn was under no legal obligation to provide medical services. This should not be interpreted as meaning that the inn had no legal obligation of any kind. Knowing that a guest is in substantial distress, an inn does have an obligation to call a physician, though the inn is not obligated for the bill. This is the guest's obligation.*

The problem here was that the inn, having undertaken to provide medical services, tendered an incompetent practitioner. Given the fact that the house physician was away, calling any doctor of the guest's choosing would have been the better recourse.

Management Ideas: Liability for Negligence

1. Review all appropriate state statutes or administrative regulations concerning:

a. fire regulations—especially fire doors, required fire fighting appliances, exits, wiring, heating plant, skylights, and fire and flameproofing requirements for Christmas trees, ballroom and lobby displays, and decorations.

b. building code—stairs, basic physical plant, handrails, safety and regular inspection of elevators.

2. The amount of liability insurance should be reviewed from time to time to take care of inflationary trends.

3. Swimming pools in inns are often considered semi-private and, as such, do not require the stringent regulations of public pools (such as city pools). However, it is considered good management to clearly mark the depths along the pool and to build a fence to keep unattended small children out of the pool area. (Remember the Attractive Nuisance Doctrine!) Although most states do not require lifeguards (and you should check state regulations), the conscientious manager will consider this question very carefully. The decision will be especially difficult for smaller operations where the wages of a lifeguard would add significantly to the overall expense of the operation.

4. Supervision should be attentive to assure that the personnel, especially housekeeping and room service, do not leave objects on floors and hallways, including unsightly room service trays full of leftovers.

5. Snow and ice should be promptly removed.

6. Observe your employees for any aggressive tendencies and violent temper. Check their previous employment for these weaknesses.

7. Train employees to recognize and eliminate dangerous conditions which might harm guests.

8. Design a simple accident form (as shown) and have it properly filled out by the investigating management personnel to aid the insurance carrier and to assist the attorney in preparing your defense to diminish damages.

9. Have the telephone numbers of manager or owner, the fire department's rescue squad, police, house physician, coroner, lawyer, and insurance broker readily available. The

supervisors should know whom to call in a given situation. Spell out each case for them as part of the operating manual.

10. Make an effort to show training films and other audio or visual training devices on the prevention and handling of injuries.

11. Get together with your insurance broker and insist that he supply you with additional material, such as handbooks, pamphlets, and checklists dealing with the whole area of liability for negligence.[1] Insist that a specialist accompany you on a tour of your property to point out weak spots. It makes good sense for the insurance company and for you.

---

1. While collecting material for this text, the authors were surprised to find that the insurer of a large hotel chain had no such material to pass on to hotels.

CHAPTER 5

The Hospitality Industry and Its Liabilities for the Property of Guests and Others

Introduction

TWO DISTINCT SETS of problems fall within the subject matter of this chapter. First, there is the unique liability that hotels and motels have for the care of their guests' property. We will consider this subject immediately below. Second, there is the more general and less onerous duty that almost anyone has when he happens, for one reason or another, to have possession of the property of another, assuming that the relationship of host-guest is not established. This is often the case, for example, when restaurants or private clubs such as country and city clubs check the coats of their patrons. It is also often the case when hotels or motels have property of persons who are not guests or who are no longer guests. This sort of relationship will be considered in the second portion of this chapter.

Common Law Liability of Hotel or Motel
for Property of Guests

The basic rule at common law is that the hotel or motel[1] is an insurer of the property of the guest. Being an insurer means that the inn is liable for the loss or destruction of the guests' property, almost regardless of the reason for the loss. Loss may occur because of theft, completely unexplained disappearance, or almost any other imaginable cause.

There are only three, relatively unimportant exceptions under which the inn is not liable for loss or destruction of property.

1. Act of God: Basically this means an extremely unusual natural phenomenon such as an earthquake, a hurricane, or a tornado. Extreme conditions of heat, cold, or wind, which are not really unprecedented, would not qualify. Obviously, an Act of God is not an important exception to the innkeepers' liability except in very unusual cases, an example of which is the following: A guest stayed in a hotel for a long period of time, and management had allowed the guest to store a large trunk in the basement. One day, during an extremely heavy, unprecedented rainfall, the basement flooded and damaged the trunk and its contents. Under the above exception the hotel was not held liable. This was a borderline case and the hotel was lucky to have won.

2. Act of Public Enemy: This emphatically does not mean an act of the F. B. I.'s "public enemy number one or two." The exception refers not to acts of criminals but to loss resulting from foreign invasion or insurrection. Obviously, this too is an exceedingly rare exception to the innkeeper's liability.

3. Negligence of the Guest: If a guest is very negligent in the care of his property, so that the loss is almost entirely the fault of the guest himself, the innkeeper will be absolved from liability. A number of cases, however, indicate that the negligence of the guest must be of a higher degree than ordinary contributory negligence. For example, a female guest staying in a hotel went to bed, leaving the door ajar for her

---

1. There is some slight authority for the proposition that motels are not held to the same strict liability as hotels. This would seem plausible, in that hotels, having a central lobby, have at least some control as to entrance and exit of strangers. Motels have virtually no control beyond the hope that guests will lock their rooms. However, there is so little authority on this question that the motel operator would do well to assume that he is liable unless an attorney familiar with the law of his state advises him to the contrary.

roommate who was out. During the night and before the roommate had returned, a burglar entered the room and stole a mink coat which belonged to the guest. The hotel was held not liable because of gross contributory negligence of the guest. The same was true when a guest left her coat unattended in the powder room where no attendant was present and where a sign expressly warned guests not to do so.

However, the fact that the guest merely left the door open is not ordinarily considered sufficient reason for the hotel to avoid its responsibility, as the following case suggests. A guest left his room temporarily and forgot to close his door. A maid had seen the guest leaving and also had seen the open door. The maid did not immediately close the door; one hour passed, and, during this hour, some of the guest's property was stolen. The hotel was held liable.

Legislative Modification of Common Law Liability

Bear in mind that we have been discussing the common law. The common law may be modified by legislation in the particular state, and often is. Moreover, many states have, in recent court decisions, departed from the traditional liability.

At present, in many states, the innkeeper bears only a presumption of liability, meaning that if he can show that he was not at fault he will be absolved from liability even though the cause of a guest's loss may remain unclear. Some states confine the innkeeper's liability to baggage, which is defined as goods brought to the hotel for the guest's convenience and use. However, most states apply the innkeeper's liability to any articles brought by the guest.

In one case, a guest brought with him two jewelry cases, which he properly deposited with the hotel. They were later picked up by a stranger under fraudulent circumstances. The hotel tried to disclaim liability saying that this was not baggage for the guest's convenience and use but merchandise. However, the hotel was held liable.

What can management do to protect itself from losses resulting from liability for guests' property? It cannot make a contract with the guest to limit its liability. Such a contract would be without legal effect, because innkeeping, a public calling, is a business which ordinarily cannot limit the liability imposed on it by law. It also cannot refuse to accept baggage and articles; aside from the common law liability, that would plainly be poor management. However, management can lessen its risk by making reasonable rules for the conduct of guests. Some suggestions will be made at the end of this chapter.

There is a common exception to the insurer's liability of the innkeeper, based upon many state statutes: If the innkeeper provides a safe for use by guests, and if he posts notices informing the guests of the existence of a hotel safe, the innkeeper will not be liable for goods that could have been placed in the safe but were not. In a typical case, a guest who had lost an article covered by the statute, but who did not comply with the posted notice, claimed that the notice of liability displayed in her room did not mention what would happen if she did not act as required. She claimed recovery for the items, but the court rejected the claim, stating that it was not necessary for the posted notice to specify the consequences of non-compliance.

Notices in many states do not have to be posted in each guestroom. A statute required the posting of notices in a "public place." The hotel did so, in posting it behind the registration desk. This satisfied the requirement.

When depositing valuables in the hotel's safe is required in order for the guest to protect himself, and the articles somehow mysteriously disappear from the hotel safe, the inn will nonetheless be liable in most states.

Only a person in authority, such as the resident manager and the night manager (not the front office clerk) should be given authority to limit liability for the hotel. This is, of course, also the case when making agreements beyond the hotel's regulations—only the person in authority should be able to do so.

Obviously, there is a good deal of variation from one state to another as to the extent of the innkeeper's liability. Probably the prudent manager should check with an attorney to determine the extent of liability in his particular state, and especially, whether by providing safe, and adequate notices, liability for small valuables may be avoided.

Commencement of Liability

Assuming that the inn bears some degree of liability for goods of its guests, which will almost always be the case, the next question is, at what point does this liability commence?

Essentially, the inn assumes liability when it begins to exercise custody and control over the property of the guest, which is not necessarily at the time of registration. This rule is easier to state than to delineate precisely. Custody and control means that there exists a power by which management can exclude others from the property and which gives management the opportunity (though it may not be exercised) to do such things as pick up the property, move it, or store it.

Normally, custody by the inn begins when the guest turns his baggage over to a bellperson or carries it himself to his room. However, a number of other possible situations may occur. Suppose that the patron obtains a reservation and sends his articles ahead by mail. He is not yet a guest, but nonetheless the inn would be liable upon receiving the property. How about the guest who simply places his baggage in the lobby? The cases suggest that if the guest deposits the baggage with someone authorized to receive it, such as the bell captain, or if he deposits it someplace indicated by the inn for guests to leave their baggage, such as the baggage rooms, the inn is presumed to have custody. The inn is usually not liable if the guest merely leaves his baggage unprotected and unwatched in a lobby, without any direction by the inn that he should do so, and without notifying the innkeeper that he is doing so.

Commencement of Liability for Automobiles

Automobiles present a particularly frequent source of problems for the innkeeper, probably because they tend to be more valuable than routine baggage. If a guest's automobile is turned over to an attendant employed by the hospitality operation or to some independent party under the direction of the operation (for example, an independent garage owner or parking lot owner), liability by the inn begins when the automobile changes hands. For example, if a hotel or restaurant employee parks a guest's car and the car is damaged, management will be held liable. In one case, a guest parked his car on the parking lot of a hotel. Some days later a drunk driver, who had no connection with the hotel, damaged the parked car. In this case, the guest could not recover damages. However, damages *were* recovered in the following case. A guest was told by the front office clerk that the hotel furnished free parking. The guest parked his car, took some articles out, and left some in the car, which he locked. Passing by the desk he told the clerk that he had left valuables in the car. Next morning the guest discovered articles missing from his car which had been broken into.

The two cases differ in that the hotel had definite knowledge that the guest had brought an automobile (and its contents) with him and, therefore, was held liable in the second case. There is a difference among the states as to whether the inn becomes liable if the guest merely parks his car in a parking lot designated by the inn for use by guests. The majority probably hold that this does not render the inn liable. There seems to be at present a greater tendency to hold motels liable in this situation.

In either case, it is inevitably held that if the inn receives the automobile key from the guest after he parks, the inn will be liable from that time for loss or damage to the car, since the keys represent custody and control in a practical sense.

Termination of Liability

When does liability of the inn for the guests' property terminate? Obviously, in the normal instance the guest and his property leave together, and the liability of the inn terminates at that time. Hence, the major question is, suppose the guest leaves property behind? In most states, the insurer's liability of the inn terminates when the guest departs, but the inn nevertheless remains liable for negligence in caring for the property. (Thus the inn becomes a bailee of the property of the guests.)

So far we have discussed the insurer's liability for hotels and motels, which is almost absolute (see the three exceptions as previously noted). Now we are going to describe the other form of liability for property, which is bailment.

Bailments and the Hospitality Industry

Aside from the unique instance in which the innkeeper has an insurer's liability for his guests' effects, normally one person's liability for care of property owned by another depends upon the law of bailments. Examples in which the hospitality operation (aside from the innkeeper's liability) may have some liability for care of property of another are: property left behind by a departed patron, property checked with an attendant at a coat room, and property entrusted to management temporarily for safekeeping, such as a diamond ring left at the front desk by a jeweler after his stay was over. (In this case the ring subsequently was lost, and the hotel held liable as a bailee, even though the special liability of the innkeeper did not apply because the jeweler was no longer a guest.)

A bailment may be defined as the "rightful possession of goods by one who is not the owner." The parties to any bailment are the bailor and the bailee. The bailor is the party owning the property who has passed possession to the bailee. (Remember the "o" in bailor as designating the owner of the property.) The party who receives the property is the bailee. As we will explain below, every bailee has some responsibility for bailed property. Thus, the hospitality operation must decide when it wishes to act as bailee.

Creation of Bailment

In order for the bailment relationship to be created, there must be some sort of delivery by the bailor and some sort of acceptance by the bailee. Of course, whether or not a bailment is created is frequently a critical question, because normally there will not be liability based on a duty to care for property unless a bailment can be found. On the other hand, once a bailment is found, the bailee will clearly have some duty to care for the bailed property, though to what extent this is true depends upon the nature of the bailment.

In summary, the main questions in the law of bailments tend to be (1) was there delivery and acceptance of the bailed article to a bailee? And (2) if so, what degree of care did the bailee owe?

Delivery and Acceptance

Many cases involve questions that arise in restaurants where coats or other property are placed in the restaurant while the owner dines. Ordinarily, this situation does not create a bailment. The owner of the property does not deliver the property by, for example, hanging a coat on a hook usually without the manager's knowledge, nor is there an acceptance arising from this act. On the other hand, if coats or other articles are deposited in a checkroom with a hatcheck person, a bailment does arise because there is delivery and acceptance.

Again, we want to underline the fact that management's provision of facilities, such as coat racks, usually does not mean acceptance. Therefore, this alone does not ordinarily create a bailment.

Mislaid or Forgotten Property

Mention was made above of the rule that the *insurer's* liability of the hotel for the guest's property terminates when the guest leaves. What, then, is the status of property left behind? A bailment is created when an employee discovers the property of the departed guest. The delivery may be unintentional, as may be the acceptance, but finding of the property by the innkeeper creates a bailment. However, if the property disappears before discovery by the innkeeper, no bailment ever came into existence, and, hence, no liability was ever fixed upon the inn. Naturally, cases arise in which the departed guest charges that hotel employees must have found and kept the property left behind. However, because the *insurer's* liability terminated, the burden is on the former guest to prove that this actually happened and that a bailment resulted. This would ordinarily be difficult.

Other Bailments

Articles deposited with the hotel by friends or business associates of a departed guest in the mistaken belief that he is still there, as well as a departed guest's letters received by mail, would constitute a bailment when accepted by the inn. Again, the liability would be only of a bailee and not of an insurer.

Restaurants and private clubs often provide parking facilities for guests. If the arrangement is merely that the patron may park, lock his car should he wish, and proceed to accept the hospitality of the firm, no bailment is created. However, if management provides carhops who park the automobile and keep the keys until the diner or member calls for it, a bailment would result. In fact, a bailment would result if arrangements were made for the guest to park his car and turn in a car key to the desk.

We noted above that when an inn provides a guest parking space, the insurer's liability of the inn usually applies. Therefore, the question of whether or not a bailment is present is not involved. If the owner of the car is not a guest at the hotel, however, there would be liability on the inn only if a bailment could be found.

Summarizing the above: whether or not a firm (other than

an inn) is liable for the property of a patron depends first upon the question of whether or not a bailment has been created. If there is no bailment, there is no duty to take care of another's property. But, even if a bailment is created, the liability of the bailor is not that of an insurer, and he is liable only in the event of negligence on his part. How much negligence must be found on the part of the bailor depends upon the particular type of bailment involved and is the next subject of discussion.

Liability of Bailee

Assuming that a bailment is found to result from a particular transaction, the traditional common law approach is to divide all bailments into three classifications: (1) Bailments for the sole benefit of bailee. This is the case, for example, where you borrow your neighbor's car or his lawn mower. This is purely to serve your own interests. For this reason, your responsibility as bailee is naturally very high. The hospitality firm will rarely be the bailee under this sort of arrangement. Most firms do not often borrow the property of others. In this sort of bailment, the bailee owes a duty of great care and is liable for only slight negligence. In common language, this means that if one is a bailee solely for his own benefit, the slightest lack of care resulting in loss or destruction of property will result in the bailee's liability. (2) Mutual benefit bailment. This is the situation where both parties gain something, the most common example in the hospitality industry being a coat checkroom. The benefit to the bailee is the small fee received, the benefit to the bailor being the security provided his coat. Most commercial bailments are for mutual benefit, and most commercial bailments are either arrangements where the bailee stores property, for a fee, or where the bailor rents property for the use of others, for a fee.

The liability of the bailee in a mutual benefit bailment is that of ordinary care, and he is liable in the event that he is guilty of ordinary negligence. Some cases illustrating this point will follow after the third point in our discussion. (3) Bailment for sole benefit of bailor, also called gratuitous bailment. This may well be the most common type of bailment in the hospitality industry. Examples are the guests leaving property behind which the innkeeper finds; the restaurant gratuitously checking coats or parcels, or the restaurant holding, for safekeeping, property left behind by a diner.

The bailee is responsible for slight care in these cases and is liable only for gross negligence.

Here are some cases which deal with the relationship of bailor (the party that owns the goods) and the bailee (the party that accepts the goods temporarily for custody and control).

A person tried to get a room in a hotel but was told by the clerk that the hotel was filled. The clerk agreed to keep the person's suitcase and to notify him in case of a vacancy. Later in the evening the traveler rented a room in another hotel and came to collect his suitcase. It turned out that the suitcase could not be found. Even though a guest-hotel relationship never materialized, a bailment was created; this bailment was for the mutual benefit of both parties and not for the sole benefit of the person who had lost the suitcase, as the hotel later claimed. The reasoning that made this instance a case of mutual benefit bailment was that the hotel had "the prospect of immediate economic gain if the space had been available." The hotel was held liable for ordinary negligence.[1]

Another example: A husband and wife had stayed at a hotel for a few days. When they checked out, they asked the hotel to hold some baggage until their return. After leaving, the husband returned to the hotel and left some cash with the clerk. He received a receipt. Some days later, the couple returned to the city, but instead of staying in the hotel (they had dinner there) they slept in their partially finished apartment. Next day the husband asked for the return of his money, but both the clerk and the money were gone. The couple tried to recover damages but were unable to do so. The court decided that no guest-hotel relationship existed because the husband (guest) had made the arrangements after his departure and that only a gratuitous bailment existed. In addition, the duty of slight care owed by a gratuitous bailee had been met.

---

1. The same type of reasoning has been used in a few states in which a restaurant provided free checkroom facilities. In these cases, instead of holding the restaurant a gratuitous bailee, it was held mutual benefit because the restaurant expected to benefit from serving a meal.

Another Test of Bailee's Liability

A more modern and more flexible test used by some states to determine the bailee's liability is simply that the bailee owes reasonable care under the circumstances (as you will recall, this is the traditional approach to determining negligence in the law of tort). Whether the bailment is for sole benefit of bailee, mutual benefit, or for sole benefit of bailor is one of the important circumstances to be considered. Naturally, under this formulation, more care would be expected of a bailee when the bailment was for his benefit than would be the case if it were for bailor's benefit. This test avoids the rather arbitrary and artificial difficulty in determining just what "gross" negligence and "slight" negligence are in a particular case.

Loss Through Misdelivery

The above analysis has been confined to the question of what duty is owed by the bailee for care of the bailed article during the bailment. However, a different question is presented in the event that the bailee turns over the property to a party not the owner, and that party disappears with the property. A bailee is practically an insurer for purposes of making sure the property is not delivered to one who is not the rightful owner. Almost without exception, the bailee is liable should loss of the property result from this happening. The message is clear: The bailee, even for sole benefit of bailor, can hardly be too careful about the proper return of the goods entrusted to him.

CASE

NORTH RIVER INSURANCE COMPANY
v.
TISCH MANAGEMENT INC.
(New Jersey 1960) 166 A2d 109

Plaintiff's proofs were that the Cohens had been guests at the hotel since December 21, 1957, and that when they returned to the room on the evening of December 24, 1957 they discovered that the coat was missing from the hanger in the closet where it had been placed by Mr. Cohen. Defendant offered proofs concerning various notices, discussed more fully hereinafter, as to the availability of a hotel depository for valuables, purportedly in compliance with R.S. 29:2-2, as amended, N.J.S.A. The action of the trial court was predicated on the view that liability of the defendant depended upon either its status as bailee of the cost or its negligence leading to the loss. It concluded there was no showing of bailment, express or constructive, or of negligence, and therefore there was no liability.

The dismissal was not in accord with the law as we discern it from the authorities. It has long been a principle of English law, accepted by most American jurisdictions, that in the absence of statute an innkeeper is practically the insurer of the safety of property entrusted to his care by a guest, exoneration being had only by showing the loss was due to an act of God or the public enemy, or to the fault of the guest himself.

Bradley Livery Co. v. Snook, does not constitute divergent authority. It was there held only that a guest leaving his horse and carriage in an open shed outside an inn without calling the innkeeper's attention to the fact or leaving the equipment with his hostler does not show the express or implied bailment which is the theoretical basis for liability of the innkeeper generally. It is implicit in the opinion of the court that the commonlaw rule of liability stated above would be cognizable in the ordinary instance of goods entrusted to the innkeeper by being brought within the premises by the guest.

Moreover, the very fact that our Legislature in 1907 chose to adopt a statute sharply restrictive of the liability of hotelkeepers to guests (see below), in common with most other American jurisdictions, is strong evidence that the common-law rule of liability was previously regarded as obtaining in this State.

It is therefore clear that defendant was not absolved by mere failure of the plaintiff here to adduce evidence of the defendant's negligence.

It remains to be considered whether, as argued by defendant, the result below should be confirmed because of the application to the facts of the case of the special statute affecting liability of hotels to guests as amended by L. 1952, c. 145, N.J.S.A. We are not called upon, in this connection, to construe these provisions IN EXTENSO, as defendant's sole reliance thereon is placed upon its alleged compliance with R.S. 29:2-2. as amended, N.J.S.A. This provision, stemming from L. 1907, c. 183, ordains that whenever a hotelkeeper provides a safe or other depository for safekeeping valuables of types specified in the act, including furs, and "shall place, in a conspicuous position in the room or rooms occupied by such guests, a notice stating the fact that such safe or other depository is provided" in which the valuables may be deposited, and a guest neglects so to deposit the articles, the hotelkeeper is not liable for loss of the property. If the goods are thus deposited the liability of the hotelkeeper for loss is limited to $500.

Defendant's principal dependence in this regard is upon a document which, according to its proofs, was left under the glass on a dresser in the hotel room at the time it was occupied by the Cohens. This paper is about 11-1/2 inches square. Commanding its top-center space, in the style of a title, is the prominent designation, "The Traymore Directory." Adorning the upper left is a picture of the hotel, described as "Center of the Boardwalk, Atlantic City, N.J." In four columns, under prominent captions, are set out the featured facilities of the hotel: "Restaurants," "Beach and Pool Facilities," "Entertainment," "General Information," and "Traymore Shops," with subcaptions and pertinent information under each. What defendant relies upon is a box of about 2-1/2 inches in the lower righthand corner of the "Directory," bearing the caption, "Notice to Guests," in type substantially less prominent than that of the five captions for featured facilities set forth in much more prominent positions elsewhere on the paper. This notice contains the statutory information concerning the availability of a "safe" and of the absence of liability of the hotel for valuables not left there.

The question before us is whether this notice satisfied the statute as a matter of law. We hold it did not. The "notice" constituted a minor appendage of what in primary purport was a hotel directory. A guest whose eye should be caught by this document might very well stop reading it as soon as he gathered its general import, if not interested therein, and before reaching the lower corner where the "notice" is set out. The express requirement in the statute that the notice be placed "in a conspicuous position" evidences an intent that the notice itself be conspicuous and a serious question is presented as to whether this notice can be regarded as conspicuous, in the light of the diverting character of the main substance of the data on the paper on which it appears.

Statutes of the kind here involved, since in derogation of the conflict with common law, are required to be strictly construed.

We conclude it was for the jury here to decide whether the notice relied upon by defendant was such a notice as to meet the statutory requirement, and also whether the leaving of it on the dresser, rather than placing it upon a door or other prominent place which a guest would necessarily see when using or leaving the room, constituted the placing of the notice in a conspicuous position in the room.

Other warning notices relied upon in this case by defendant did not constitute compliance with the statute, whether because lacking in the full statutory information, not being left in the room, or not being placed in a conspicuous position therein.

Evidence of actual knowledge by the guests of the availability of a hotel depository and of the limited statutory liability, is, by the weight of authority, with which we agree, not an acceptable substitute for strict compliance with the statute as to notice by the hotelkeeper.

Reversed and remanded for a new trial.

* *There have been many cases essentially like this case, and the moral is simple. Although a large number of states do have statutes whereby the innkeeper is relieved from his common law liability as insurer, the innkeeper is relieved of this liability only if he follows the appropriate statute exactly. Here, the innkeeper did not provide satisfactory notice of the presence of a hotel safe. Consequently, he was not relieved of his duty at common law, just as if the statute limiting his liability did not exist.*

CASE

FRANK A. GILLETT v.
WALDORF HOTEL COMPANY
(Wash. 1925) 241 P 14

ASKREN, J.— This is an appeal from a judgment of the court denying recovery in an action to recover for valuables, lost while guests of a hotel.

The facts follow: Appellants, in August, 1923, registered at respondent's hotel, and were assigned to room 333. Retiring that evening at 10:30, both appellants tried the door of their room to ascertain if it was locked. The door was fitted with what is commonly known as a Yale lock, with a flat key being used for the purpose of entering the room. The lock had what is known as a spring catch which does not require the use of a key to open the door from the inside. The door was fitted with no other form of lock, and there was no other way by which the door could be locked, bolted or secured from the inside, which would prevent a person having a key from entering the room.

Before retiring, Mr. Gillett hung over the bathroom door his trousers, which contained a wallet with $90 in money. Mrs. Gillett removed from her fingers some diamond rings and laid them on a dresser. Upon arising next morning, it was found that both the money and the rings had been taken. Investigation showed that the catch or bolt in the lock had been pushed back and was held by the spring, indicating that it had been unlocked by the use of a key, there being no marks of violence. Complaint was immediately made to the hotel management and detectives were assigned to the case. Investigation was made with regard to the door and the room in general, the detective and manager of the hotel and other persons being in the room that morning.

Upon the trial of the case, there was no dispute as to the facts which we have just stated. But respondent, the hotel, sought to exempt itself from liability upon the ground that appellants were guilty of contributory negligence, and upon the further ground that it had complied with 6862, Rem. Comp. Stat., as follows:

"No hotel-keeper, whether individual, partnership, or corporation, who constantly has in his hotel a metal safe or suitable vault in good order and fit for the custody of money, bank notes, jewelry, articles of gold and silver manufacture, precious stones, personal ornaments, railroad mileage books or tickets, negotiable or valuable papers and bullion, and who keeps on the doors of the sleeping-rooms used by guests, locks or bolts, and who keeps posted in each of said sleeping rooms a notice of liability as hereinafter specified, shall be liable for the loss or injury to such property suffered by any guest unless such guest has offered to deliver the same to such hotel-keeper for custody in such metal safe or vault and such hotel-keeper has omitted or refused to take it and deposit it in such safe or vault for custody and to give such guest a receipt or claim check therefore: *Provided, however,* That the keeper of any hotel shall not be obliged to receive from any one guest for deposit in such safe or vault any property hereinbefore described exceeding a total value of one thousand dollars, and shall not be liable, for any excess of such property, whether received or not: *Provided further,* Such hotel-keeper may by special arrangement with a guest receive for deposit in such safe or vault any property upon such terms as they may agree to in writing, but every hotel-keeper shall be liable for any loss of the above-enumerated articles of a guest in his inn or hotel after said articles have been accepted for deposit, if caused by the theft or negligence of the hotel-keeper or any of his servants."

We have heretofore held that exemption from liability by virtue of this section can only be had by strict compliance with the statute, and that the notice required by the statute must be given exactly as provided. We have also held that, when the relation of innkeeper and guest and the loss of goods have been established, the true rule is that the innkeeper is *prima facie* liable, and the burden is on him to show such facts as will exonerate him. *Watt v. Kilbury,* 53 Wash. 446, 102 Pac. 403.

Both Mr. and Mrs. Gillett testified positively that they made search of the room to ascertain if there was any notice posted therein as provided by the terms of this act. They testified that they had traveled much, and knew that such notices were common. The only testimony contradicting this is the statement of the manager that he saw the notice in the room that morning. The trial court, in its memorandum opinion, expressed grave doubts in regard to the testimony offered on the question of this notice, but finally made a finding to the effect that the notice was posted as required by law. It appears from the testimony that a number of persons were in the room that morning, and it seems strange that, if the notice was there, no other witness testifies to having seen it. It must be apparent that, when this loss was claimed, the manager would at once realize the importance of having the notice in the room, and would have called the attention of either appellants, the detective, or some employee to the fact that the notice was there. It appears that these notices were tacked upon the wall near the telephone. It is common knowledge that such notices are liable to mutilation and destruction, and for that reason many hotels place them under glass and securely fastened to the door or some other part of the room. When it is remembered the ease with which such a notice can be destroyed, and when it is further considered that, outside the manager, not a single employee of the hotel or any other witness testified to the fact that this notice was in the room, we think it can safely be said that respondent has not met the burden which the law imposes upon him to show that he has complied with the statute, and that it was error for the court to so hold.

The trial court, also, found that appellants were guilty of contributory negligence because the money was left in the trousers hanging over the bathroom door, and the rings placed upon the dresser instead of placing them under their pillow or in some other place of like character. But in this we think the court was in error. Guests have the right to assume that the room to which they are assigned is a safe place. . . .There is no rule of law requiring guests to secrete their valuables within their room in order to free themselves from a charge of negligence.

It is contended by respondent that, even if there was no notice in the room, there was a notice printed on the page of the register where appellants registered for the room, which stated that the hotel kept a safe for the keeping of cash and jewelry of guests; but there was no evidence in the case to indicate that appellants saw this, and their testimony upon this point was positively that they did not. It is not common for guests upon registering to read printed matter upon the page of the register, and the evidence here leads irresistibly to the conclusion that appellants did not know of, or see, this notice. It has been held in a number of jurisdictions that where the statute requires the notice to be posted in every room the printing of the notice at the head of each page of the guests's register is not enough. Thus in *Nesben v. Jackson* . . . it is said:

"A guest, in signing a hotel register, is not bound to assume that he is signing a contract, and read everything printed in the register or on the page he signs;" citing *Murchison v. Sergent, supra,* and *Olson v. Crossman,* **31 Minn. 222, 17 N. W. 375.**

The evidence showed that the value of the rings and money taken was in excess of $1,600. The statute expressly limits the liability to $1,000. Statutes limiting an innkeeper's liability have generally been upheld by the courts. . . .There is no claim made here that the loss comes under the latter portion of the statute where the liability is not limited if the loss is caused by the theft or negligence of the hotelkeeper or any of his servants.

The judgment is reversed, with instructions to enter judgment in favor of appellants in the sum of $1,000.

TOLMAN, C. J., HOLCOMB, FULLERTON, and MAIN, J. J., concur.

---

* *Under the statute quoted here, liability by the innkeeper could be limited, but in order to claim the benefit of the limitation, the inn had to comply exactly with the statutory requirements. This they failed to do.*

Obviously, leaving his belongings about a room when the room is locked would not constitute contributory negligence of the guest.

Management Ideas: Liability of Guest's Property

1. Check on existing state statutes which might limit the liability of management. Carefully follow all instructions to the letter. If notices are required on "entrance doors" to guest rooms, do not put up notices on the bathroom door. If notices are required in "public places," do not put notices at the far end of hallways, etc. If the statute requires that the notice include mention of the consequences when valuables

are not deposited in the safe, management must comply with the regulation. If the statute requires that guests notify management if their valuables exceed a certain sum, a receipt may be issued to a new limit.

(read)

TABLE 3–LIABILITY FOR

19.48.030 Liability for loss of valuables when safe or vault furnished—Limitation. Whenever the proprietor, keeper, owner, operator, lessee, or manager of any hotel, lodging house, or inn shall provide a safe or vault for the safekeeping of any money, bank notes, jewelry, precious stones, ornaments, railroad mileage books or tickets, negotiable securities or other valuable papers, bullion, or other valuable property of small compass belonging to the guests, boarders, or lodgers of such hotel, lodging house or inn, and shall notify the guests, boarders or lodgers thereof by posting a notice in three or more public and conspicuous places in the office, elevators, public rooms, elevator lobbies, public corridors, halls or entrances, or in the public parlors of such hotel, lodging house or inn, stating the fact that such safe or vault is provided in which such property may be deposited; and if such guests, boarders or lodgers shall neglect to deliver such property to the person in charge of such office, for deposit in the safe or vault, the proprietor, keeper, owner, operator, lessee or manager, whether individual, partnership or corporation, of such hotel, lodging house or inn shall not be liable for any loss or destruction of any such property, or any damage thereto, sustained by such guests, boarders or lodgers, by negligence of such pro-

Above is a sample of a "Limitation," this particular one from the State of Washington.

Under Number 1 is defined who is responsible for safekeeping, e.g., proprietor, keeper . . . of hotel . . . Number 2 spells out what is covered. It is interesting to note that railroad tickets are included but not airline tickets. (This suggests that some changes in the statute might be overdue.) Number 3 defines the guest, and Number 4 clearly explains where the notices of this "Limitation" have to be placed.

Front office personnel must be trained to issue such receipts properly. Be certain that personnel refrain from making promises that might be understood by the guests as waiving the limitation.

LOSS OF VALUABLES

prietor, keeper, owner, operator, lessee or manager, or his, her, their or its employees, or by fire, theft, burglary, or any other cause whatsoever; but no proprietor, keeper, owner, operator, lessee or manager of any hotel, lodging house or inn, shall be obliged to receive property on deposit for safekeeping exceeding one thousand dollars in value; and if such guests, boarders or lodgers shall deliver such property to the person in charge of said office for deposit in such safe or vault, said proprietor, keeper, owner, operator, lessee, or manager, shall not be liable for the loss or destruction thereof, or damage thereto, sustained by such guests, boarders or lodgers in any such hotel, lodging house, or inn, exceeding the sum of one thousand dollars, notwithstanding said property may be of greater value, unless by special arrangement in writing with such proprietor, keeper, owner, operator, lessee or manager: *Provided, however,* That in case of such deposit of such property, the proprietor, keeper, owner, operator, lessee, or manager of such hotel, lodging house, or inn, shall in no event be liable for loss or destruction thereof, or damage thereto, unless caused by the theft or gross negligence of such proprietor, keeper, owner, operator, lessee, or manager, of his, her, their, or its agents, servants or employees.

It not only says "public and conspicuous places" but also explains what is understood under this concept. Suits have been filed for exactly that reason: a failure by the lawmakers to properly define locations. Number 5 is perhaps the heart of the limitations: a dollar amount is given (in this case $1,000). Number 6 explains that the innkeeper is liable only in case of theft or gross negligence. Other causes, such as fire, are ruled out.

TABLE 4–SAFETY

WESTERN SERVICE AND SUPPLY

OLYMPIC HOTEL*

SAFETY DEPOSIT KEY RECORD

KEY NO.	DATE ISSUED	ISSUED BY	AUTHORIZED

As a condition of the receipt of such articles deposited by me in this safety deposit box, I hereby agree that access to this safety deposit box will be obtainable only through this signature and upon the presentation of this key in person, and for any failure so to present the key in person the Olympic Hotel shall not be liable for any loss occasioned by such failure to personally present such key. And I hereby agree that, in the event I should not personally surrender this key and remove the contents of this box within ten (10) days after I shall cease to be a guest of this Hotel, the Olympic Hotel may force entrance to said safety deposit box and remove the contents thereof, and while retaining the said contents, the Olympic Hotel shall not be liable for any loss occasioned by my failure to remove such contents, and in any such event or in the event that the key is lost while in my custody I hereby agree to pay to the Olympic Hotel the sum of Ten Dollars ($10.00) for the cost of opening the safety deposit box and replacing the key.

NAME .... ROOM NO. ....

HOME ADDRESS ....

*Courtesy of the Olympic Hotel, Seattle

DEPOSIT KEY RECORD

IDENTIFICATION CARD SAFETY DEPOSIT

Signature	Date	Time

I hereby surrender my key to Box No._____ and hereby certify that all property placed or stored therein has been withdrawn therefrom and is now in the owner's full possession, all claims against and liability of the Olympic Hotel being waived accordingly.

NAME ....

Date.............................. Cashier's Initials...............................

This form (see facing page for opposite side) attempts to control the access of the guest to his safety deposit box. It also limits the right to use the box after departure to 10 days.

TABLE 5—SAFETY

SAFETY DEPOSIT ENVELOPE

DO NOT DETACH UNTIL PACKAGE IS CALLED FOR

A **DEPOSITARY'S CHECK**

THIS CHECK TO BE SIGNED
WHEN PACKAGE IS DEPOSITED
Deliver to OWNER ONLY AFTER SIGNA-
TURE on DEPOSITOR'S Check "B" is wit-
nessed and compared.

N.º 1728

Signature of Depositor _____

Received by _____ Date_____19___

B **THIS CHECK FOR DEPOSITOR**

N.º 1728

Depositor to sign this check ONLY when
package is called for and in the presence of
the Clerk on duty. Package will be delivered
only to party originally depositing it, whose
signature appears on Depositary's check on
package.

Signature of Depositor _____

Received by _____ Date_____19___

This form (see facing page for opposite side) is used for the disposition of small, valuable packages, such as those containing jewelry.

DEPOSIT ENVELOPE

DIRECTIONS

When Depositor has filled and sealed the envelope, it is required that he sign his name on the Depositary's check A. The clerk who receives the package must also sign his name on Check A, and date it.

Detach Depositor's check B, and deliver to him as receipt.

When Depositor calls for his package, have him sign his name on Depositor's check B. Then to prove ownership the clerk will compare it with the signature on Check A. If satisfactory, the clerk will sign, date and detach check A, deliver the package, then file checks A and B for record.

Packages too large for the envelope may be checked by detaching both coupon checks; follow signature directions above; attach check A to package, and give check B to depositor.

Form #228
W. W. Wilcox Mfg. Co.
Chicago 6, Ill.

Management Ideas:
Protecting the Property of Guests and Others

1. With the help of your attorney, formalize and publicize reasonable rules for guest conduct with regard to handling of room keys and luggage, closing of guests' doors, and displaying of valuables.

2. Install self-closing devices on guest doors. The failure of guests to keep their doors closed does not always absolve management from its liability.

3. Establish procedures to protect guests' luggage while guests are registering. Management is usually liable for loss at this time. Use chains or nets to secure the luggage in the lobby. For luggage temporarily stored, use a 2-part claim check, at no cost to the traveler. This produces more security for the guests' luggage and carries less liability for management. Have the luggage room closed at all times and see that the key remains with the bell captain or front desk. Any check-in or check-out with a bellperson should be recorded as to time, mode of arrival or departure, taxi number (if any), number and description of luggage, room number, and bellperson's initial. (See Table, facing page)

4. In addition to maids, whose movement on guest floors is normally determined by housekeeping needs, and bellmen, whose movement is controlled by the bell captain or front office, every other employee's movements should be controlled. Room service employees can be controlled by a room service record book (which could be used at the same time to control the clearing of china, glasses, etc., from the floors) and employees of the engineering staff by a similar record book (which could serve at the same time for the handling of maintenance orders). *Every* movement of *any* employee to or on guests' floors should be controlled.

5. When employees check out, a strict parcel control should be instituted with parcel checks issued by department heads. A separate policy for taking magazines from vacated guest rooms and out of the premises should also be considered. The safest policy is not to allow any magazines to be taken out. This simple procedure may be important!

6. Until we have wider use of no-key locks, guests should be asked to identify themselves when picking up their room

TABLE 6

69606 DATE____
PIECES____

STORAGE TAG

NAME____

ITEM____

CHECKED BY____

WILCOX/STANDARD   CHICAGO-PHOENIX

STORAGE TAG
CLAIM CHECK
69606 DATE____
PIECES____

"In consideration for storage of the property covered by this check, the owner or person depositing same agrees:

The custodian is not liable for loss or damage to the said property as a result of fire, theft, ordinary or gross negligence, or otherwise, unless it shall appear that the loss or damage was caused by willful act or misappropriation on the part of the custodian or his employees.

If the property is not called for within ten days, the custodian shall have the right to make reasonable charge for its storage, or within six months, the custodian shall have the right to sell the property under its lien for unpaid charges or as unclaimed property."

CHECKED BY:____

CUSTODIAN:____

key. For example, after a guest has said, "I would like the key for Room 1214," the room clerk should ask, "May I ask your name?" or something similar.

7. Strict control over the number of room keys for each room at the desk should prevail (two probably being the limit). Locks should be changed immediately if a key is missing. Strict control of the keys used in housekeeping can be ac-

complished with the help of a key control book and a large key board. The issue of master, general master, and grand master keys should be done with great care. A large hotel of an international chain did not know how many general master keys were issued and to whom. Management did not think it possible to have one of the general master keys duplicated. It took one of our students 10 minutes and 25 cents to have one key duplicated and presented to a surprised management.

8. Make arrangements with every locksmith, dimestore, department store, and whoever else uses a key copying machine in your vicinity not to duplicate any of your keys. Not that this procedure will prevent the crooked employee or guest from getting a duplicate—it only limits the odds somewhat. Print DO NOT DUPLICATE on all keys.

9. Telephone operators should never give out the room number of a guest. The operator should always ask, "Should I connect you with Mr. Brown?" Let Mr. Brown give his room number to his friends. The same procedure should rule the front office staff as well.

10. A non-guest should never be sent to a room without the guest being contacted by the front office staff and then only if the guest requests the visitor.

11. Special care should be taken at night to keep the lobby and elevators under observation.

12. Make it part of the general employment contract that employees have to report and deliver all lost and found property.

13. Set up clear procedures for handling of lost and found, which should include a lost and found book (with numbered pages) and a locked room or locker. Only one person, either from housekeeping or front office in a hotel or the manager of the restaurant or club, should be responsible for the content of the lost and found room or locker. Procedures should further include specific instructions as to how and how often to contact guests and the way items should be identified by guests.[1]

---

1. To avoid embarrassing guests, some hospitality operations do not notify guests of articles left in rooms. The operation simply waits until the guest makes an inquiry. In some jurisdictions, a sale is required in an open and advertised auction as prescribed by statute for lost and found, abandoned checkroom articles, and skipper baggage.

14. Instruct employees to refer guests to management when questions of liability arise.

15. It is important for hotels,[1] restaurants, and clubs to consider whether or not they want to be liable for guests' automobiles. If the operation wishes to avoid liability, self parking should be the rule. Hotels might even refrain from asking for the license number on registration cards.

16. Restaurants and clubs will have to decide if they want to be liable for guests' coats. If so, they should hire an attendant who does nothing else but guard the coats. If they wish to avoid liability when providing coat facilities in entrances and powder rooms, they should post a sign disclaiming liability. One club uses a device where the member inserts a dime and locks his coat on a hook. A key is dispensed at the same time. When the member returns for his coat, he inserts the key, and his coat and the dime are returned. This gives the member better protection for his coat and at the same time avoids making the club a bailee as there is no delivery to any agent of the club. Unfortunately, management must discourage buspersons and waitresses from accepting guests' coats to be hung up as this may result in being a bailee.

17. Give contact employees some authority to adjust auto damage and theft of articles from automobiles before the guest departs. This may be done through an adjustment of his account, which may save correspondence and further legal problems.

---

1. Motels will be held liable in most cases.

TABLE 7

RIDPATH HOTEL, INC. - SPOKANE, WASHINGTON

ACCIDENT REPORT*

DATE_____

GUEST'S NAME _____ ROOM NO._____

AUTOMOBILE MAKE AND MODEL_____

LICENSE NO._____ STATE_____

PARKING TAG NO._____ TIME OF DAY ACCIDENT OCCURRED_____

PRIOR EXISTING CAR DAMAGE_____

_____

_____

COMPLETE EXPLANATION AS TO HOW CAR WAS DAMAGED:_____

_____

_____

_____

_____

_____

DETAILED AND COMPLETE LIST OF DAMAGES:_____

PARTS:_____

_____

_____

_____

PAINT AND MATERIAL:_____

LABOR:_____ TAX:_____ TOTAL:_____

If Hotel Cannot Obtain Estimate of Repair Costs, Guest is Requested to Mail Estimate
to Hotel for Authorization.

Signature of Employee _____

Guest Acknowledges Above List of Damages to be the Full Extent of Hotel Liability.

_____
Guest Signature

*This form from the Ridpath Hotel is used for guests' cars
damaged in the hotel's garage.*

*Courtesy of the Ridpath Hotel, Spokane

CHAPTER 6

Liability Based on Food or Beverage That Is Contaminated, Spoiled, Adulterated, or Contains Foreign Objects

RESTAURANT AND CLUB operators have to be scrupulously careful to avoid serving contaminated food and drink. Illness, or even nausea (caused by a cockroach found in one's dinner), may result in an action of negligence; more likely an action will be based upon warranty. In that event the requirements of negligence, especially the careless act, need not be proved.

The most common form of warranty action is based upon the Sales section (Section 2) of the Uniform Commercial Code. Sales of food and beverage by restaurants are specifically enumerated as constituting sales, although prior to almost universal adoption of the UCC this point was considered debatable. Another section of the UCC provides that an implied warranty of merchantability attaches as a matter of law to every sale. Essentially, this means that every sale of prepared food in a restaurant carries with it a guarantee that it is fit for human consumption according to normal standards. Breach of this warranty is basis for a lawsuit, assuming, of course, that the defect in the food or beverage is sufficiently serious to warrant the expense of litigation.

In a suit based on warranty, negligence need not be proved; all that need be proved in order to recover damages are the warranty, which is a matter of law, the breach of warranty, and damages. Obviously, under these circumstances a restaurant could be liable for food purchased and prepared by others and even that purchased in cans, or in the frozen state.

A number of states have held that a seller of food will not be liable for foreign objects of a nature that one would reasonably expect to find in the food. Bones in many types of fish or meat would be a normal adjunct of a serving. So would seeds in cherries, olives, or grapefruit. However, if a seller or manufacturer advertises or labels his wares as "boneless" or "seedless," this statement will usually constitute a warranty that the goods are as described, and may result in liability even when the food is of a type naturally containing the bone or seed.

Management Ideas: Foodservice Sanitation for Guests and Employees[1] Read

1. Have all plans for new construction or major remodeling of food and beverage preparation and service areas approved by the proper environmental health authorities.

2. Use only food supplies from approved sources. Approved sources means, e.g., approved oyster beds or wild game farms, instead of game from a hunter friend. If you are in doubt about a product, always select the product which comes from out of state; it has been federally inspected.

3. All foods in storage, being prepared, displayed, served, sold, or transported have to be protected from contamination. Store all perishable foods at safe temperatures (45°F. or below, or 140°F. and above). Require foodservice employees to observe strictly all rules of personal hygiene. Hold perishable foods out of the hazardous temperature range (45° to 140°F.) Use sneeze guards on buffets. Require rubber gloves for certain work on food. Observe proper thawing procedures for frozen foods (reject any frozen food package which shows a heavy

---

1. It is beyond the scope of this text to present a complete enumeration of all the federal regulations in detail. Therefore, a broad discussion of the main areas will follow.

accumulation of ice on the outside of the package—it has been thawed and refrozen). Insist on washing of fresh fruits, vegetables, and meats before preparation.

4. Make sure that none of your employees work while affected by any disease in a communicable form, while a carrier of such disease, while afflicted with boils, or while afflicted with infected wounds, sores, or an acute respiratory infection. This rule is imposed by OSHA. (See chapter 12.)

5. See to it that all equipment and utensils are designed in such a way that they are easily cleanable, which means quite often that the equipment can be taken apart easily. All equipment bearing the seal of approval of the National Sanitation Foundation (NSF) is designed with this purpose in mind. Cutting boards and meat blocks, if made from wood, are especially difficult to clean. Use hard rubber cutting boards. Clean all china, glasses, and silver in an appropriate dishwasher, observing proper temperatures, and store all equipment and utensils in clean places. Use common sense to observe proper housekeeping practice.

6. Use only water which comes from approved sources. Provide proper and adequate toilet facilities for your guests and employees (OSHA) as well as handwashing facilities in the toilet area and in the kitchen. These facilities should have disposable towels or an air-dry machine. Pay special attention to proper garbage disposal and to rodent and vermin control. Buy an extermination contract, but make sure that your exterminator is skilled and reputable.

7. The construction of floors, walls, and ceilings should be such that they can be well maintained. Provide adequate storage for employees' clothing and proper changing facilities. A foodservice employee should not enter a kitchen in street clothes. Keep the operation neat, clean, and free of litter and rubbish. Establish cleaning routines and check at irregular intervals with the help of a check-off list.

8. You are responsible to your guests for the content of canned and frozen foods. Deal only with reputable companies.

9. If you accidentally serve a piece of a metal scratcher in your homemade soup, you are liable to your guests for any damages. If the guest finds a piece of bone in food where bone would be expected, as in T-bone steak or fried sole, you

are not liable. Instruct your personnel to look out for foreign objects in food and beverage.

10. What can you do if a guest complains about an upset stomach because he ate yesterday in your restaurant? Establish the exact time of his meal and all of the items of the meal, including any side dishes. Also ask for his exact symptoms, e.g., sweating, vomiting, headache, etc. Certain foodborne illnesses require certain foodstuffs and particular times to develop (time of onset), and chances are that he did not get sick in your operation. Provide yourself with the necessary material from the local environmental health administration so that you can ask intelligent questions and offer reasonable explanations. If the guest still insists on litigation, call your attorney or insurance company.

CHAPTER 7

Contracts

Introduction

THE CONTRACT IS the most important and the most basic form of business transaction. Anyone who has reached adult life has made many, perhaps hundreds, of contracts, probably without ever becoming involved in legal difficulty. For example, a private person buys a car, signs a lease, buys groceries. The hospitality operator makes a contract every day with each of his guests; he buys from his suppliers and signs land and building leases. However, the possibility of important legal consequences arising from misunderstanding the law of contracts is always present, and the hospitality manager needs to be thoroughly familiar with some principles of this area of the law.

A contract may be simply and precisely defined as "an agreement enforceable at law." One will immediately note that this definition includes two important notions. First, a contract is based upon an agreement of the parties. The parties themselves determine what the terms of the agreement will be and decide whether the terms are acceptable. Only when they have indicated their assent to the terms will a contract result. Second, once made, the contract is enforceable; that is, either party breaking the contract can in all probability be successfully sued by the other party.

It is the fact that contracts may be enforced through court action that makes this area of study important. Simply put, the hospitality operation must have established procedures for determining that the agreements intended to be enforceable will result in legally binding contracts. At the same time, it is important for management to avoid committing itself to a contract if it has not yet reached the decision to be bound.

THE AGREEMENT

Apparent Assent

The statement was made earlier, "Only when they have indicated their assent to the terms will a contract result." The question is, how do courts determine whether parties have indicated their assent?

Some readers may respond, that if the contract is in writing, the agreement is enforceable; otherwise it is not. THIS IS A COMMON MISUNDERSTANDING. Most oral contracts are enforceable. An oral contract is more difficult to prove than a written contract, but if there is evidence sufficient to convince a jury of the contract's existence (such as a witness or even convincing testimony by the party claiming it), the oral contract will be binding. (Exceptions are considered later in this chapter under "Form.")

The test by which courts measure whether parties have made an agreement is "apparent assent." That is, if a party conducts himself in a manner that would lead a reasonable man to believe he has agreed, he is held to have agreed in fact.

This test is used simply because no one can determine what other people are really thinking, but we all make judgments based on what they say and how they act. The test, then, is not actual intent (which cannot be known) but apparent assent which we can all judge.

The issue of apparent assent becomes important in cases where one party was joking and the other was not. . .if the joke was sufficiently persuasive, a contract will result. . .or in cases where one party assented because he misunderstood or was mistaken, which was not known to the other.

The point was made that contracts need not be written to be enforceable. However, it is true that if a contract is signed, the fact of a party's having signed is almost invariably evidence of his apparent assent to contract. Therefore, it must be admitted that questions involving apparent assent are usually confined to oral contracts. *a request for something*

Offer and Acceptance

The most important technical requirements of a contract are that there be an offer by one party and an acceptance by the other. Both the offeror and the acceptor must, of course, appear to mean what they say; that is, they must manifest their assent as discussed above. A valid offer contains two parts: (1) a promise and (2) a request for something in return. For example, I will provide my banquet room for your convention for three days (the promise) in return for your paying $500 (the request). To accept, the other party must simply agree unequivocally to the terms of the offer. Thus, the reply "I agree," or "It's a deal," would be an acceptance of the above offer.

An offer does not remain effective forever. It may be revoked (that is, cancelled) by the offeror any time before acceptance. Or, it may be rejected by the other party; as soon as this occurs the offer is legally terminated. A counter offer, in which the offer is met with a different offer, usually a somewhat lower price, is considered a rejection, which nullifies the original offer and at the same time presents a new offer to the offeror which he may accept. Example: Management offers to a prospective guest convention facilities for three days for $500. The guest responds: "I'll give you $400." Management may drop the matter and could not be bound by his offer at $500 since it was rejected. On the other hand, management could accept the offer at $400 and, thus, make a binding contract.

Offers may also be terminated by some clause contained within the offer, such as, "this offer is good only until November 1, 1975," or, if no specific time limit is set, by expiration of a reasonable period of time as determined by a jury.

Often it happens that before parties to a business transaction formally declare their position by binding offer and acceptance, they carry on extended negotiation in which their discussions are in hypothetical terms. This process is normal and useful but presents one problem: the possibility of confusing a hypothetical proposition with a binding legal offer. If the parties have agreed in advance to reduce their ultimate agreement to writing, the problem will not arise; otherwise, the only advice is to be clear as to whether a proposition is merely bargaining or whether it is indeed intended as a firm offer.

The instant a valid offer is accepted, a binding contract results, and from that instant neither party may revoke or reject. From that time the parties must perform or risk being sued for breach of contract.

Certainty

As a matter of common sense, it is obvious that even when two parties have manifested their assent to contract and have exchanged offer and acceptance, a valid contract cannot result unless the terms are sufficiently definite that normal people, or, if necessary, judge and jury, can ascertain what the terms of the contract were intended to mean. In short, a contract must be sufficiently definite and certain so that it can be interpreted as a contract.

Essentially, this subject may be terminated with the advice: be very careful to make certain that the contract is sufficiently clear and precise so that an independent party, knowing nothing about the contract, will be able to understand its terms. If the contract meets this criterion, it should pass the test of certainty.

There is one especially important trap for the unwary in the area of contract law. This is the agreement to agree. Businessmen who have difficulty in working out the hard details of a bargain often are tempted to take the easy way out and provide "such facilities as will be agreed upon at a later date," or "at a price to be agreed upon later." These provisions would result in no contract at all! Agreements to agree in the future result in no contract. Either the parties agree with one another or they do not and when they merely plan or hope to agree, they clearly have not yet reached a certain agreement.

One form of agreement to agree *is* enforceable, however. This is when a sale of personal property is involved. Personal property means any form of moveable property; for example, food, beverage, hotel room furnishings, or anything bought in stores or shops. A sale of personal property means the transfer of ownership of moveables for a price, usually money.

When a contract to sell personal property is arranged, the contract may be valid even though the parties have not yet agreed upon the price or other terms. If later the parties are unable to agree, the courts will usually determine a reasonable price and enforce the contract.

Form

The point was made earlier that most contracts, even those that are oral, are enforceable. However, some are not. We include here a discussion of those contracts that must be written to be valid.

This is a technical and dull subject; it is simply not practical to treat it exhaustively. We will simply enumerate those types of contracts which must be in writing and will omit a detailed discussion.

1. Contracts for purchase or sale of real property. Real property means land, building, or anything permanently attached to land or buildings. No matter how definite you and the other party are in your agreement, until the matter is reduced to writing (and most states require other formalities such as notarization and/or witnesses), the contract is not binding.

2. Agreements by one party to pay the debt of another. A guest has run up a large hotel bill, but another person calls up and says, "let him stay there—I'll guarantee the tab." You cannot hold the other person responsible unless you have his promise in writing.

3. Agreements that will not be performed within one year. An association makes arrangements for a convention to be held two years hence. This agreement is unenforceable unless it is in writing. Or, you may have agreed with a sub-tenant to lease premises for over one year. Again, this must be in writing. There are some borderline cases and exceptions to this rule, but you should err on the side of getting the agreement in writing when in doubt; you can always check with your attorney to be certain.

4. Contracts for purchase or sale of personal property of $500 value or more. Personal property, you will recall, is anything moveable. There are a number of exceptions to the general rule. If payment has already been made and received by the seller or if the seller has delivered the merchandise to you, the contract is legally binding; but bear in mind that you

still have to prove somehow that there *was* a contract. The rational policy is to make certain that all contracts for personal property of $500 value or more are in writing, rather than worrying about possible exceptions.

Aside from the question of what contracts have to be in writing to be enforceable, there is the additional question: what is the *effect* of a contract being in writing, whether it has to be or not?

The general rule is that a written contract cannot be contradicted by oral testimony. In other words, if you sign a contract and get into a dispute over some provision that you consider to be unfair, your oral statement that the contract did not really mean what it plainly says will normally not be admissible in court. There are fairly extensive exceptions to this general rule, but, obviously, in terms of "preventive medicine," the only advice possible is: make certain you are sure you agree to the terms of the contract before you put it in writing and sign it.

Problems in Actual or Legal Assent

Earlier, the question of apparent assent was discussed. When two parties have exchanged offer and acceptance, and have each appeared to assent to the agreement, a contract is formed.

We will now explore some qualifications to this proposition. Suppose that two parties make a contract by which one reserves certain banquet facilities on a certain night. The agreement is perfectly clear in an objective sense, but the party making the reservations simply does not understand the nature of the arrangement for reasons that are entirely his own fault—he forgot his glasses and is too embarrassed to mention this fact. Assuming he makes an agreement under these circumstances, he will be bound even though seriously mistaken. This is an example of a unilateral mistake, which results when one party misunderstands a contract, and the other party does not.

Ordinarily, unilateral mistake is no defense in a contract action, and the mistaken party is bound. The main exception is when the other party realized that the first was making a mistake and took advantage of him. This is usually difficult to prove; but if proved, the mistaken party will be able to escape the contract.

In rare instances both parties to a contract are mistaken.

For example, hotel or restaurant facilities might be leased when, unknown to either party, the facilities had been destroyed by fire. Both parties assumed the existence of the facilities, and both were mistaken. Under these circumstances, the contract would be considered as nonexistent. The rule is that when both parties to a contract are mistaken as to some essential aspect, a contract never came into being.

Suppose an association negotiates a contract providing that 1,000 members will use various inn facilities for a convention. The inn negotiates a special rate because of the large volume anticipated. Actually, only 250 members appear, and later it can be shown that the association never really expected more. In short, they secured the contract through intentional, false statements, which resulted in financial losses to the inn. This is an example of fraud. Assuming that the inn can prove that the representations made were both intentional and false, it can recover money damages for its loss. As a general rule, any contract where assent by one party is secured through intentional, false statements and where damages result provides the basis for recovery in fraud.

What if the poor attendance was not intentional, but merely the result of a bad guess? Assuming that there was no contractual provision requiring a minimum guarantee (which would have been a good idea by the association), this would not constitute fraud but merely misrepresentation. Misrepresentation is identical to fraud except that there is no intent to deceive. Money damages usually cannot be recovered for innocent misrepresentation. If the hotel is alerted to the situation in advance, it may escape the contract. Here is one example of what can happen. An association contracts for 500 rooms (with a special lower room rate), and only 350 members show up. An enforceable contract exists, and the hotel can collect for 500 rooms at the agreed-upon room rate. But probably management would prefer to void the old contract on the basis of misrepresentation and negotiate a new contract for the 350 rooms, possibly at the normal room rate.

Disability

Certain classes of people may manifest their assent to a contract, after a fashion at least, but nonetheless will not be held to their assent for reasons of social policy. There are two main categories of such cases: first, those with some sort of mental impairment and second, minors, who are not held responsible as a matter of law.

Not much need be said about the first category. Guests at an inn who extend their stay while so inebriated or so incapacitated by drugs that they are not rational may usually avoid such contracts. However, for services consumed under circumstances in which the management was unaware of the disability, they may usually be held.

The majority of states consider a person to be a minor until he or she is 21, but an increasing number of states have reduced the age of majority to 18. A minor may avoid most of the contracts he or she is likely to make; however, there is authority to the effect that a minor can be held to his or her contract for lodging at an inn. The minor presents a difficult problem to the restaurant or club because he can ordinarily avoid a contract made for restaurant food or for services of a club. On the one hand, it is probably not good public relations to categorically exclude minors from all club and restaurant facilities. On the other hand, there is the remote chance that the minor will complete his meal and refuse to pay. To put it bluntly, he can probably get away with it. However, chances are that such losses will be rare.

When there is a question of renting expensive facilities, such as a banquet hall, to a group of minors, for example, a fraternity or scout troop, the best course would be to insist upon an adult cosigner who is known to be reliable.

Illegality

The basic rule concerning contracts that involve illegal activities is simple. Such contracts are absolutely unenforceable. Courts cannot be put in the embarrassing position of assessing damages because someone failed to perform his side of an illegal contract. The result is that if one is not paid what is owing on an illegal contract, the money is hopelessly lost.

There are three areas in which the hospitality industry would most likely be party to an illegal contract: liquor violations, gambling, and prostitution. We assume the reader is not involved in any of these, but if he is, he must be aware that he cannot rely upon legal action to collect accounts due.

There are exceptions to the rule, whereby an innocent, unknowing party might be able to collect. However, the better policy is to be circumspect and avoid any involvement in the above-mentioned activities.

Consideration

Mentioned under the heading of "Offer and Acceptance" was the statement that an offer must contain (1) a promise and (2) a request for something in return, while an acceptance must contain an unequivocal assent to the request in the offer. This means that almost every contract contains promises by both parties.[1]

In fact, for the contract to be binding, both promises must contain something of substance. The term for the substance in each of the promises is consideration. Thus, in every contract, each party must promise to do something he was not previously required to do. In the hospitality industry, of course, this normally means that one party promises to pay money and the other to provide services of some kind.

Usually there is no problem as to whether or not consideration is present. However, it is important to remember that if consideration is not present a promise cannot be enforced. Gratuitous promises without an agreement that something will be provided in exchange are unenforceable and can be ignored.

Having received a large amount of business from an association, the manager of the hotel assures the president of the association that it may use a banquet room on a complimentary basis. The manager resigns, and the new manager refuses to honor the agreement. The agreement did *not* constitute a contract because there was no consideration, and the new manager may cancel the agreement. Favors or patronage rendered in the past do not qualify as consideration. In every contract the consideration must relate to something to be done by each party in the *future*. However, mutual promises to do something in the future will constitute consideration and may, of course, be legally enforced and money damages awarded by the court.

Special Situations

One question that might arise is when an inn advertises "Rooms $12.00 and up." All of the $12.00 rooms are rented,

---

1. Occasionally an offer to contract is made so that it can be accepted only by doing something. For example, "I'll pay you $50 *when* you finish painting my fence." Painting the fence is the acceptance. These contracts, termed unilateral contracts, include only one promise, but this type of contract is fairly rare.

but a party insists upon being provided a room at that price. Is the inn obligated to provide a room for that price merely because of the advertisement? The answer is no. Advertisements are considered invitations to trade; that is, the ad is an invitation for the traveller to come in and make an offer to transact business at the terms stated. The innkeeper may then decide whether he wishes to accept the traveller's offer. Of course, as has already been noted, the inn has a legal obligation to accept all well-comported applicants. However, it need not accept them at the minimum rate if all rooms that normally rent for the minimum rate are full.

Suppose an inn advertises a minimum rate when in reality they have no rooms at all going for that rate. This is surely unethical, and many states have consumer protection legislation that would be violated by such a practice.[1] The inn could be subjected to criminal prosecution or civil liability for engaging in such a practice in these states. But, nothing is going to make an innkeeper liable merely because he advertises rooms at a certain rate, fills all the rooms that normally go for that rate, and offers to let out a higher-priced unit.

Mention was made earlier about confirmed reservations. Ordinarily, contract principles apply to this situation, and such contracts are enforceable by either party. There may be a substantial problem of proof if the reservation is made over the telephone.

Principles similar to the advertisement of the inn apply to the restaurant menu. Again, this is an invitation to trade, and the offer is made by the diner who selects a particular bill of fare. Just as the inn may not have a vacancy at a particular advertised rate, the restaurant may have run out of a particular item on its menu but would nonetheless not be in breach of contract.

A Simple Contract Form for Use With Associations

One of the most significant types of contract made by the hospitality operation in terms of the amount of money involved is likely to be a contract to provide services for an association. A simple contract form appears on pp. 117-119.

---

1. Some states even prohibit displaying room rates in corporate names, e.g., "Motel 6."

FORM I

HOTEL
Banquet and Private Functions Contract

☐ Patron

☐ Banquet Mgr.

Dated _____

AGREEMENT between _____ HOTEL, hereinafter called the "Hotel" and _____ hereinafter called the "Patron".:-

Name in full of Patron _____

Principal Address _____   Tel. No. _____

P.A. System _____   Spotlights _____

Date of Function: _____   Hours from _____ to _____

Nature of Function: _____

Room or rooms to be used _____   Rental _____

Minimum number of persons guaranteed _____   Price per person _____

Contract must be signed and returned by: _____

The Menu:

Other Charges:

_____   Total $ _____

(*cont.*)

Note that this contract is, if properly filled out, definite as to the obligation of each of the parties, and that the consideration to be extended by each party is set out. There could be no reasonable question as to whether there was agreement as to offer and acceptance.

FORM I (Cont.)

1. IT IS FURTHER AGREED that the charge for room reserved shall be paid for upon the execution of this contract; and that Patron will pay the balance due for services and accommodations hereinabove agreed upon 48 hours in advance of the function, or at the option of the Hotel. Patron will execute and deliver a written guarantee satisfactory to the Hotel for the payment therefore.

2. Patron agrees to advise the Hotel in writing at least 48 hours in advance of the definite number of attendance at the function, which in no case shall be less than the guaranteed minimum; but Hotel shall not be responsible for service or accommodations to more than 10% increase over said minimum guaranteed attendance.

3. THIS CONTRACT IS SUBJECT TO THE TERMS AND CONDITIONS PRINTED ON THE REVERSE SIDE HERE AND EXPRESSLY MADE A PART HEREOF.

ACCEPTED:

_____ HOTEL

Patron _____ By: _____

(1) All federal, state, and municipal taxes applicable to this function shall be paid for separately by the Patron in addition to the prices herein agreed upon.

(2) No beverages of any kind will be permitted to be brought into the Hotel by the Patron or any of the Patron's guests or invitees from the outside without the special permission of the Hotel, and the Hotel reserves the right to make a charge for the service of such beverages.

(3) Patron agrees to begin its function promptly on the scheduled time and agrees to have its guests, invitees and other persons vacate the designated function space at the closing hour indicated. The Patron further agrees to reimburse the Hotel for any overtime wage payments or other expenses incurred by the Hotel because of Patron's failure to comply with these regulations.

(4) Hotel reserves the right to exclude or eject any and all objectionable persons from the function, or the Hotel premises, without liability.

(5) Patron assumes responsibility for any and all damages caused by it or any of its guests, invitees or other persons attending the function, whether in rooms reserved, or in any other part of Hotel.

(6) It is understood that Patron will conduct its function in an orderly manner, and in full compliance with the rules of the Hotel management, and with all applicable laws, ordinances and regulations.

(7) Patron agrees not to put up any displays within the Hotel without the written permission of the Hotel.

(8) Patron agrees to obtain the services of Union Musicians and entertainment.

(9) In the event that Hotel, at request of Patron, furnishes any food, beverages, or any other services not provided for in this contract, Patron agrees to pay Hotel the charges therefor as soon as bill is rendered, and if not so paid the said charges will become due under this contract even though not specifically provided for in this contract.

(10) In the event of breach of this agreement by Patron, the Hotel reserves the right to cancel same without notice, and without liability to the Patron. The amount paid by Patron for use of space shall be retained by the Hotel as and for liquidated damages; but this shall not preclude the Hotel from recovering its actual damages sustained by reason of any breach hereof.

(11) THIS AGREEMENT IS CONTINGENT UPON THE ABILITY OF THE HOTEL TO PERFORM THE SAME, and is subject to strikes, labor disputes, accidents or other causes beyond its control; and in any such event, the Hotel shall not be liable beyond the amount paid for the use of the rooms herein reserved. If the room reserved herein cannot be made available to the Patron for causes beyond control of the Hotel, the Hotel reserves the right to substitute similar or comparable accommodations for the function, which substitution shall be deemed by Patron as full performance under this agreement.

(12) This agreement is not assignable.

FORM II

Suggested Letter of Agreement for Convention or Meeting to be Written on Association or Facility Letterhead

Developed by the American Society of Association Executives in cooperation with representatives of the hotel industry.

Note that this is only a suggested format. It should be adapted by the association or facility to meet its needs. The important requirement is to reach agreement on each service area and execute a written statement of such agreement. This suggested letter is not prepared for convention center use; the booking of these convention facilities requires a quite different approach.

Dear Sir:

This will confirm the arrangements made by

_____ and _____
    (hotel representatives)   (association representatives)

concerning the _____ forthcoming
meeting/convention.   (organization or group)

The _____ hereafter referred to as the

"Association" and _____ Hotel/Motel hereafter referred to as the "Facility" agree that:

1. The association hereby engages the facility and its staff for a meeting/convention and the facility agrees to furnish same on the following terms:

    (a) Scheduled dates and days of meeting/convention from _____
        to _____ .

    (b) Start exhibit set-up _____ A.M./P.M. _____
                   (hour)   (date)

(c)   The rates to be charged by the facility for sleeping rooms are as follows:*

Single Room from \$ _____ to \$ _____ or Flat Rate _____

Double Room from \$ _____ to \$ _____ or Flat Rate _____

Twin Room from \$ _____ to \$ _____ or Flat Rate _____

Suites from \$ _____ to \$ _____ or Flat Rate _____

Other from \$ _____ to \$ _____ or Flat Rate _____

(d)   The association presently estimates the number of room required to be as follows:

No. of Single _____ minimum and _____ maximum

No. of Double _____ minimum and _____ maximum

No. of Suites _____ minimum and _____ maximum

No. of Other *(specified)* ___ minimum and _____ maximum

(See suggested Penalty Clause Terminology — Appendix A). Note: If room rate is from X to Y dollars (paragraph c) then specify number at *each rate.*

It is anticipated that _____ of those attending may wish
$\qquad\qquad$ (number)

to have an earlier check-in. The dates for early check-in are _____ ,
in which case the facility will provide rooms therefor at convention rates specified.
The same rates will apply for___days following the convention/meeting.

The facility guarantees it will provide at least the maximum number of rooms set forth in paragraph (d) and the association agrees to provide occupancy for the minimum number of rooms specified.

The association agrees to keep the facility informed periodically of registrations received in advance so that more exact estimates can be made as to the room requirements. It is agreed that periodic changes in the above estimates (d) may be made from time to time prior to the meeting/convention, but in no case shall the minimum or maximum number set forth in this agreement be changed except by written agreement. The association and facility shall agree in advance on a mutually satisfactory review schedule of convention developments and specify when and how rooms may be released by either party. (Review dates and times should be specified in this letter of agreement.) After the agreed upon cut-off date(s) the association and facility will be held responsible to meet the final agreement.

Facility agrees to refer all requests for suites (if all are held) and/or public rooms to association for approval before assignment if the applicant is identified with the association or industry it serves.

The association shall/shall not request room deposits of convention delegates.

The facility agrees to provide the association with a final occupancy report showing number of rooms occupied each day of the convention period. (See Appendix B)

(e)   It may also be incorporated in this contract an agreement by the facility to improve, remodel, or create certain rooms or areas or add services prior to the event covered by this contract. The specifics of the changes in the facility should be spelled out in this contract and failure to meet the requirements by a specified date would be cause for cancellation of the agreement by the association without penalty. Reasonable and adequate notification to the

*By mutual agreement in writing, these rates, as well as the rates set forth in paragraph 1(f) hereof may be revised or otherwise changed.

(cont.)

FORM II (Cont.)

association should be required of any remodeling which would result in a change in the number of suites or public space available.

(f)   Anticipated meeting room requirements:

Room Reserved	From Date & Hour to Date & Hour	Type of Function Anticipated	Rental Charge, if any
_____	_____	_____	_____
_____	_____	_____	_____

A tentative schedule of meeting rooms required will be submitted to the facility at least___months in advance of the meeting/convention. A firm and detailed schedule of meeting rooms required will be furnished the facility not later than__ months before the meeting/convention. Unless otherwise specified in this agreement, public space as outlined above shall be reserved for the association unless released in writing. (If total facility is being booked the language should state "All public space shall be reserved for the association without charge (or with charges as specified) for use at the discretion of the association.)If the association is utilizing only a part of the facility, the above room schedule should be completed.

(g)   Anticipated exhibit space required. The facility agrees to reserve_____ rooms for use as exhibit space. Cost for space shall be_____(if any).

Services to be provided in exhibit hall by facility include_____

_____

_____

_____

_____

_____

(here specify such items as cleaning, extra lighting, carpeting, advance storage, security, number of microphones available, audio visual equipment available, operator rates, power supply, or other items agreed upon.)

The facility warrants that the following union regulations prevail in the exhibit hall and will promptly notify the association of any change. Current conditions are: (outline union requirements in exposition hall.)_____

_____

_____

(h)   Special equipment needs of the association:
      Description and rates:

_____

_____

_____

(i) A guarantee of the number of persons attending each food or beverage function will be given to the facility at least ___ hours in advance of the function. The facility agrees to set for ___ % over the guarantee. The above food functions (package) shall be provided at a per person cost of $_____. Beverage/liquor by drink and/or bottle shall be provided at a cost of $_____. Such prices are subject to review up to six months prior to the event.

If a meal function is to be added to the package, the price applied shall be the same as that included in the above package for a like meal.

(j) The following complimentary accommodations will be furnished by the facility to the association.(Description of rooms and suites, dates of availability and numbers.)

_____

_____

_____

_____

_____

_____

_____

(k) The facility will give the association notice of any construction or remodeling to be performed in the facility which might interfere with the event. In such event, facility must provide equal alternate space within the facility under contract.

2. The facility and association agree that the following procedure shall be followed with regard to gratuities

_____

_____

(Note — specific individuals, amount or % and procedure may be spelled out.)

3. It is agreed by the parties that the foregoing sets forth the essential features of the agreement between the parties and that *specific details* as to registration, rooming of persons attending, handling of material, special services, collection of tickets, accounting, master account charges, promotion publicity and other matters will be worked out in writing to the satisfaction of both parties prior to or during the meeting/convention and generally following the procedures set forth in the Convention Liaison Manual published by the Convention Liaison Committee, 1101 16th Street, N.W., Washington, D.C.

4. This agreement will bind both the association and the facility and except as above provided in paragraph 1(e), may be cancelled by either party only upon the giving of written notice at least_____(years)(months)(days) prior to the dates of the meeting/ convention or no later than_____(specific date). It is further provided that there shall be no right of termination for the sole purpose of holding the same meeting/convention in some other city or facility.

5. The facility and the association *each* agree to carry adequate liability and other

(cont.)

FORM II (Cont.)

insurance protecting itself against any claims arising from any activities conducted in the facility during the meeting/convention.

6. The performance of this agreement by either party is subject to acts of God, war, government regulation, disaster, strikes, civil disorder, curtailment of transportation facilities, or other emergency making it inadvisable, illegal or impossible to provide the facilities or to hold the meeting/convention. It is provided that this agreement may be terminated for any one or more of such reasons by written notice from one party to the other.

Yours very truly,

_____ (Association)

By_____ Chief Elected
Officer (title)

_____ Chief Paid
Executive (title)

Accepted:

_____ (Hotel) (Motel)
By_____ General Manager
_____ Sales Manager

*For associations using more than one facility, a similar contract should be executed with each property.

Note: Appendix A may be added to cover over-booking situation.
Appendix B is a suggested reporting form for use by the facility.

APPENDIX A

Penalty Clause Terminology (may be inserted in paragraph 1d)

In the event the facility does not provide the maximum number of rooms specified in this contract and rooms are needed by the association, the facility shall at its own expense secure comparable nearby accommodations and provide at its expense transportation to and from such rooms. This shall apply to each day during which maximum rooms are not provided and delegates must be housed elsewhere.

If the minimum number of rooms finally agreed upon are not occupied by the association, it shall upon audited proof that the rooms were not occupied and were held available for association occupancy, reimburse the facility at the agreed upon single occupancy rate for each room for each date not occupied. (American Plan arrangements will not include food in reimbursement arrangement.)

APPENDIX B

Hotel Report Form

Following the convention or meeting the facility should be instructed to furnish the association all data with respect to its use of the facility. It is suggested that the facility agree to furnish the information at the signing of the contract. This information is important for the planning for the next convention or meeting and will give valuable information for negotiating future contracts or agreements.

POST CONVENTION REPORT

ASSOCIATION NAME _____

HOTEL NAME _____

Room Rates in Effect

CONVENTION DATES_____   Single_____

Double_____

ROOMS BLOCKED_____   Other_____

1. List for each convention day room occupancy by type.

TYPE	DATES				
Single					
Doubles					
Extra Occupants					
Parlors					
Comps.					
Average Rate					
Room Revenue					

(cont.)

FORM II (Cont.)

II. List for each convention day number of —

DATES

Arrivals					
Cancellations					
No-Shows					
Check Outs					

III. Complete the following for each meal function.

FUNCTION (meal or reception & date)	GUARANTEE	PLATE COUNT	TICKETS COLLECTED (if any)

IV. List room service revenue, for association hospitality suites.

DATE   REVENUE

_____ $ _____

_____   _____

_____   _____

_____   _____

V. List the following exhibit detail.

   a.   Number of booths _____

   b.   Net square feet _____

   c.   Comments _____

       _____

       _____

       _____

Completed By _____

Title _____

A More Complex Contract Form[1]

Contract Form I incorporates all the provisions that would ordinarily be required in providing accommodations for an association. As was also true with Form I, if signed by both parties, there could hardly be any question as to whether the parties have manifested their assent to the contract or whether there is a valid offer and acceptance. Moreover, if care is used in filling the blanks, there could hardly be a question as to certainty of terms.

Providing that the association's representative is above legal age and sober when he makes his commitment, there will be no question as to mental or legal disability. The consideration is spelled out in the terms of the contract and could hardly present a problem.

Other questions, not dealt with in this form, might be the source of difficulty. Conceivably, a manager might wish to include additional provisions dealing with:

1. Right of the inn to maintain order should this be necessary at any time.

2. Provision for deposit against use of facilities, if this would not be too bad for business. (Most inns do not require this, but occasionally cancellations occur that result in serious losses.)

Management Ideas: Contracts

1. Overbooking, whether accidental or intentional, is not a valid reason for not honoring a confirmed reservation. In such an event, a contract exists on which the hospitality operation could be held liable.

2. Watch out: while remedies for breach of contract are normally confined to out-of-pocket expenses, in rare cases they have included damages for emotional distress and disappointment.

3. Management is faced with a dilemma in maintaining reasonable occupancy (given the problem of no-shows), while at the same time avoiding overbooking.[2] If the guest is not able to appear, but he informs you of this somewhat in advance, a reasonable effort should be made to rent the room;

---

1. Both forms were supplied through the courtesy of the American Hotel and Motel Association.
2. See cases on this subject in chapter 2.

if this is done, then the deposit—less any expenses—must be returned.

4. Include a limitation in written confirmations made without deposits to the effect that, "the reservation will be held until 6 p.m. unless notified."[1]

5. Restaurant managers should also be sure to honor reservations. If the guest's name appears on your reservation list, a contractual obligation probably exists; if the guest requests service and is ready, willing, and able to pay a reasonable charge, he should be seated and served. Instruct your personnel, especially those who take reservations, which guests, if any, you do not want to serve, in order to avoid an unwanted contract (for example, with a party who has bad credit standing and is likely to want to charge). A restaurant has that right, unlike an inn.

6. Make sure you insert in your catering contract a phrase by which change (decrease or increase) may be made in the number of covers, within certain limits. For example, "up to 48 hours before the function a change in covers of 15 percent can be made; 24 hours a change of 5 percent can be made."

7. Do not take a guest's word that his company or relatives will take care of the bill; insist that he have such a promise in writing. Clip the letter to the guest's folio. It may prevent an embarrassing situation.

8. When a minor checks in, your duty remains to receive him. However, you can ask for pre-payment.

---

1. If management is concerned about goodwill, it might put in a provision saying that "in case the hotel is filled, management will provide comparable accommodations at no additional expense at a nearby hotel."

CHAPTER 8

Who Has Authority to Contract on Behalf of the Hospitality Operation

Introduction

SUPPOSE THAT THE manager of an inn contracts to provide services for a convention of an association. The manager leaves the inn's employment several months before the convention is scheduled, and he is replaced by another manager. On reviewing the inn's outstanding commitments, the new manager disapproves of the contract with the association and notifies the group that the contract must be renegotiated or it will be cancelled. He justifies this ultimatum on the basis that he was not responsible for the contract, saying that the manager who drew up the contract on behalf of the hotel is no longer employed there. Consequently, the hotel cannot be held to the contract.

Is the new manager correct? Almost certainly not. But, suppose the contract had been made by the night manager who happened to be on duty when the association called? Could the hotel be held in that event? In this case the new manager would be correct in claiming that the hotel could not be held.

Clearly, the question of who is able to make binding contracts on behalf of the hospitality operation is of paramount importance.

Terminology of Agency Law

The preceding examples deal with the field of law known as agency. In exploring this area of the law, it is necessary at the outset to develop some new terminology. An *agent* is someone with the power to make contracts on behalf of someone else, who is termed the *principal*. When the agent makes a contract for his principal, obviously there is another party who is known simply as the third party. In the first example, the hotel is the principal for whom the manager was the agent, and the association was the third party.

It is not unusual for contracts to be made on behalf of a principal by an agent in the hospitality industry, or elsewhere in the business world. Many hospitality operations are corporations, meaning that ultimately the principal is not a person at all but a corporate charter in some government office. The board of directors, the president, and all the lower echelon executives are agents of the corporation in their dealings with third parties. The higher level agents, of course, delegate progressively smaller powers to other agents to deal with third parties as one goes down the organizational chart.

Authority of the Agent

The agent is viewed as a conduit of the authority of the principal. Thus, if the principal has granted the agent authority to act, and the agent makes a contract on behalf of the principal, the principal is bound. This is why in our first example on page 129, the hotel would be liable on its contract with the association. A change of agents after a valid contract is made would have absolutely no effect at all on the contract. In our second example, a night manager would almost certainly not have been given authority to contract for convention services; hence, no contract would result unless the manager ratified it, which is a subject we will explore later.

The critical question in most problems involving agency is the amount and the type of authority granted the agent by the principal. That is because the immediate problem is usually whether or not the principal can be held to the contract made by his agent. Authority of some sort must be held by the agent in order for him to bind his principal.

Real Authority

Authority to contract is divided into a number of classifications. The first major class is real authority. Real authority encompasses the situation where the agent actually does have the grant of authority he claims to have; for example the catering manager has authority to book conventions, and the room clerk has authority to contract with guests for rooms. Real authority is subdivided into two classes: express authority and implied authority.

Express authority embraces the cases where the agent's authority was conveyed to him by specific language, either written or oral. As a matter of good practice, hospitality firms will convey authority to their agents in writing, usually as part of a job description.

Implied authority embraces the cases where the agent's authority is conveyed to him by circumstances. For example, a manager has had an assistant for five years who knows the manager's duties thoroughly. The manager becomes ill, and the assistant steps into his job. No one thinks to give the assistant manager any oral or written statement of what his authority is, but it is assumed by all that he does what the manager does, and he acts accordingly.

Authority by necessity is a special form of implied authority in which the authority to contract is implied as a result of unusual circumstances, usually an emergency. For example, a bus load of people is stranded in a blizzard near a motel. The bus is stalled. The bus driver, who under normal circumstances is not an agent at all, would have the implied authority to act on behalf of his principal, the bus line, to make arrangements for lodging his passengers to prevent their freezing to death. Or, a guest with a confirmed reservation arrives late at night and, due to circumstances beyond the guest's control, cannot be put in a room in the price category he requested. The night clerk, not being able to consult higher authority, places the guest in a higher priced room than originally confirmed. The night clerk would be presumed to have authority in this case, assuming it was a reasonable and necessary alternative.

When any of the above forms of real authority are involved, the principal is bound to the contract. The question is not whether the agent used bad judgment and made a bad contract, which, of course, is bound to happen sometimes. The only question is, was the contract in fact within the agent's authority as discussed above. If so, the principal is bound to the contract whether he likes it or not. Moreover, the agent is not legally liable on losses resulting from such a contract. Of course, he might be fired or demoted or otherwise disciplined for using bad judgment, but he could not be held legally liable for resulting losses.

Apparent Authority

The major classification of authority aside from real authority is *apparent* authority. While real authority—express or implied—encompasses cases in which the agent really does have the authority he claims to have, apparent authority encompasses cases in which the agent does not actually have authority, but where the principal makes it *appear* that he does. In such cases, the agent's contracts will be binding even though he lacked real authority to contract and, in fact, was probably acting contrary to his orders.

As an example, assume that a hotel chain, a very large competitor in the convention business, hires an agent to travel around the country and discuss the chain's convention facilities with business, professional, and fraternal groups. Joe, the agent, is under strict orders merely to gather facts and provide information, but for reasons of prestige, his principal wishes Joe to *appear* to have the authority to contract. If asked, the hotel chain would always state that Joe can negotiate a contract if conditions are right. A third party, believing this to be true because the principal said it was true, makes the hotel chain an offer through Joe. Joe, believing it is now or never, and that the offer is too attractive to pass up, signs a contract for the chain even though he knows he lacks the real authority. Would the contract be enforceable against the chain? The answer is yes, because even though Joe lacked the *real* authority he did have *apparent* authority.

It is of paramount importance to remember, however, that apparent authority can stem only from some act or, at least some omission, of the principal. The agent's word alone as to what his authority is will not create apparent authority.

As an example of an omission resulting in apparent authority, consider the following actual case. A guest entered a small hotel and rang the bell. A man appeared behind the desk, signed the guest in, and accepted his valuables. Next morning the guest demanded his valuables back. Not only were his valuables gone but so was the so-called desk clerk. It turned out that the desk clerk was actually a lodger at the hotel and had no other connection with it. The hotel was held liable for the loss of the valuables on the theory that through its omission in leaving the desk unattended, it created a situation whereby a reasonable man would be deceived into believing that the lodger was the desk clerk. If you stop to think about it, this is not so unreasonable. Do you often ask desk clerks for their credentials? In effect, the court held the desk clerk-lodger was clothed with apparent authority owing to the negligence of the hotel, even though he was not an employee at all.

Although apparent authority must stem from some act or omission of the principal, to some extent what is customary in a particular business can be an important factor. For example, a manager is normally thought of as having the authority to hire and fire, purchase necessary supplies on credit, and make contracts concerning the use of the operation's facilities. If a manager should be allotted less than the usual authority, he would still have apparent authority to conduct business as most managers do, even though he lacked the real authority. In other words, contracts made by the manager would be valid even though they are unauthorized, because the title "manager" itself carries a certain amount of apparent authority.

What is the purpose behind the rule of apparent authority, which seems to carry such hazards to principals? The question is, could business function at all if the law were otherwise? Without the rule of apparent authority, anytime that you made a contract with an agent, that contract could be broken. The principal could merely claim his agent lacked authority. But the rule of apparent authority provides that if the agent seemed to a reasonable third party to have authority, because of something the principal did or omitted, then the contract within that seeming authority would be binding.

This rule is probably the only rule a sane society could adopt. Otherwise it would be too easy to avoid contracts made by agents, and no one would know whether he could depend upon his agreement.

Most third parties bringing suits in contracts probably base their claim on apparent authority of the agent rather than real authority for one good reason. When the third party attempts to hold the principal on a contract and the principal denies the authority of the agent to have made the contract, the third party has no very good means of establishing what the agent's authority really was—whether it was real or apparent. That is a private matter between principal and agent. However, if the third party can show that the principal created the *appearance* that the agent had the authority, it is irrelevant whether or not the agent had real authority. Apparent authority is enough to bind the principal. Hence, the third party is likely to confine his efforts to proving apparent authority.

When an agent misrepresents his real authority, but makes a contract that is within his apparent authority, he may be held liable for damages by either the third party or the principal. Therefore, it is a dangerous practice for the manager or any other agent to exceed his authority. Principal and agent have mutual legal responsibilities to one another.

The main duty of the agent is unwavering loyalty to the interests of his principal. Especially, he must avoid conflicts of interest, i.e., situations in which he is representing the interests of more than one principal. He may be held legally liable for damages if found to be doing so. In the hospitality industry some principals and agents are apt to be bound by contract which provides that the agent exert his efforts on behalf of principal and that the principal agrees to compensate the agent financially. Of course, such contracts must be honored by both parties. The principal owes the agent reimbursement for funds expended on the principal's behalf unless the contrary is agreed.

What lessons does the foregoing discussion hold for the manager in the hospitality firm? First, be specific as to what, if any, authority to contract is held by each subordinate. Include such a statement in each job description. This should eliminate questions as to whether in a particular case a subordinate held implied authority. Second, take pains not to create an appearance that a subordinate has more authority then he actually has been granted. At the same time, one must recognize that a subordinate will be assumed to have the usual authority of one in his position in the industry. Should you prefer that your subordinate have less than the normal authority for one in his position, a difficult situation exists; about all you can do is carefully indoctrinate the subordinate so that he will not make contracts that are in excess of his *actual* authority.

CASE

KANELLES v. LOCKE (Ohio, 1919) 12 Ohio
Appellate Reports 210

. . .We think that she by her voluntary act, or by her negligent act, had placed someone in a position where it would appear to anyone coming in to become a guest at the hotel that he was properly in charge, and that therefore she had made herself by her conduct responsible for his acts, acting with the apparent scope of a clerk or employee in a hotel, to receive property of her guests. . . .

D. Kanelles brought an action to recover the sum of $744, being the amount of money and valuables that he deposited with a man in charge of the Hotel Ohio owned and operated by Mrs. Ida J. Locke, the defendant, in which action he failed.

It seems that Mrs. Locke was running the Hotel Ohio, in 1627 Prospect Avenue, Cleveland; that on the 23rd of December, 1918, at the hour of one o'clock in the morning, Mr. Kanelles applied, with a friend, and was received as a guest in said hotel, and paid the sum of $2 for a room, to which they were assigned; that in the hotel were notices posted as is required of innkeepers under the law of Ohio; that after they were shown to a room Kanelles told the man who appeared to be in charge, and who showed them to the room, that he desired to leave his money and valuables with the hotel proprietor for the night, whereupon they all returned to the office and the man in charge wrote out a receipt describing $484 in currency, a diamond stickpin and two checks for $5 each; that the man signed this receipt with the name of the proprietress of the hotel, Mrs. Locke, by him, and gave it to Kanelles, after which he, Kanelles, retired; that in the morning he presented the receipt to Mrs. Locke and requested the return of his money and valuables, whereupon he learned that this man who apparently was in charge of the office was not in the employ of Mrs. Locke at all, and, as she claimed, had no authority to receive the money or valuables; that upon going to the room of this man Mrs. Locke found that he had absconded, taking the money and valuables with him; and that Mrs. Locke refused to make good the loss to her guest and the action was brought, resulting in a verdict for the defendant.

We have gone over this bill of exceptions carefully, and it shows that this man who signed the receipt, J. C. Clemens, was and had been for some time a roomer in this hotel. We further find that the hotel was open to receive visitors at this time in the morning, or night, and that no one was in the office to take charge of guests who might arrive except this person Clemens and a young lady who was also a boarder or lodger in the hotel; that when the plaintiff entered with his friend and asked for a room, Clemens, who appeared to be in charge, got up and went behind the counter, had them register, got the key from its proper place, assigned them to a room, and took them to their room; and that after they had gone to the room, when the plaintiff requested that the hotel take charge of his valuables, they went down to the office, and with the help of the young lady wrote a receipt which at first was not satisfactory, and then wrote the receipt of which the following is a copy:

Mr. D. Kanalos, Man in Room 111 Gave me I Diamond pin and $484.00 in bills and 2 $5.00 checks.

Mrs. Locke
Hotel Ohio
per J. C. Clemens.

During this time the only person who appeared in charge of the office was this man Clemens. Whether Mrs. Locke had turned over the office to him to do these things we are not able to determine; but the fact remains that he was the only person there, apparently in charge of a public office that was receiving guests at that time in the morning or night, and that plaintiff became a guest and had a right to turn his valuables over to the hotel for safe-keeping, in accordance with the notices published in the hotel. We think the plaintiff was warranted in believing that this man in charge was the duly authorized agent for the purpose of receiving guests and receiving for safe-keeping valuables of the guests.

It is claimed by the defendant that this man was not her agent and had no authority to receive valuables or do anything around the hotel, and that therefore she was not responsible for any money or valuables that might be deposited with him. We can not acquiesce in this doctrine. An agency may be created by estoppel, and that estoppel may be allowed on the ground of negligence or fault on the part of the principal, *upon the principle that when one of two innocent parties must suffer loss, the loss will fall on him whose conduct brought about the situation.* 2 Corpus Juris, 462, and cases cited.

Here the proprietress of his hotel left this man in the office either designedly or negligently, clothed with apparent authority to do what hotel clerks usually do, and one who came in for the purpose of becoming a guest, and did become a guest, might reasonably conclude that he had *apparent* authority to do what clerks under similar circumstances would have a right to do.

In *Curtis v. Murphy*, 64 Wis., at page 4, we find this doctrine:

A traveler who goes to a hotel at night and finds a clerk in charge of the office, assigning rooms, etc., has the right to assume that such clerk represents the proprietor and has authority to take charge of money which may be handed him for safe-keeping.

And in that case the supreme court of Wisconsin held the hotelkeeper responsible under circumstances similar to those in the case at bar.

In the case at bar Mrs. Locke, the defendant, had complied with all the requirements of the statute to relieve innkeepers from liability by posting the notices required by law, and we think that she was an innkeeper within the meaning of the law; we think that she by her voluntary act, or by her negligent act, had placed someone in a position where it would appear to anyone coming in to become a guest at the hotel that he was properly in charge, and that therefore she made herself by her conduct responsible for his acts, acting with the apparent scope of a clerk or employee in a hotel, to receive property of her guests; and we think the court was clearly wrong in holding that there was no responsibility and in rendering a judgment against the plaintiff for costs. For these reasons the case will be reversed and remanded to the municipal court for further proceedings in accordance with law.

Judgment reversed, and cause remanded.

DUNLAP, P. J., and WASHBURN, J., concur.

---

* *This case, discussed earlier in the text itself, illustrates more than one important fact. To begin with, although normally we think of one holding apparent authority as one who is an agent but is exceeding his authority, here that was not the case. The party with apparent authority had no official connection with the inn at all, aside from being a roomer. In addition, there* *had been no intentional act on the part of the management bestowing apparent authority upon the party. The apparent authority resulted merely from the negligence of the innkeeper in leaving the desk unattended. However, it is surely true that a reasonable person approaching a person behind a hotel desk would assume that person to be the desk clerk. As we mentioned before, how many times have you asked a desk clerk, a restaurant cashier, a person at the ticket window of a theatre to produce credentials before you transacted business with them?*

CASE

SOUTHERN ELECTRICAL CORPORATION v. ASHLEY-CHICOT ELECTRICAL COOPERATIVE, INC. (Arkansas, 1952) 251 SW 2d 813

Appellant, the Southern Electrical Corporation, Inc., is engaged in selling among other things, materials such as cables and accessories for electrical installation, and appellee, The Ashley-Chicot Electrical Cooperative, Inc., is engaged in furnishing electricity to homes in the counties indicated by its name. This suit was brought in the Circuit Court of Ashley County by appellant to recover the sum of $2,406.32. After the introduction of all the evidence both sides asked for an instructed verdict, whereupon the Court, sitting as a jury, found in favor of appellee, hence this appeal.

An outline of the facts and circumstances out of which the litigation arose is as follows: On December 29, 1948, Pentecost, who at that time was and for several years previously had been manager of appellee, ordered from appellant, at a price agreed on between the two, a quantity of conductor or cable including accessories. On January 11, 1949, this order was shipped by appellant, under invoice number 3723 which referred to appellee's order number 00035. It was received by appellee in due course, and it was paid for in full on the 20th by company check in the amount of $11,374.60. Following this, other shipments were made and paid for in like manner. One such shipment of material, which precipitated this controversy, was made on May 6, 1949, amounting to $8,519.69, which is not questioned in any way by appellee, but on May 13th its board of directors instructed its new manager (who had replaced Pentecost) to deduct the amount of $2,406.32 and to remit only $6,113.37, all of which was done that same day. Appellant refused to accept the check as payment in full and brought suit as stated above.

Appellee's reason for withholding payment of the balance of $2,406.32 due on the May 6th shipment involves the issues in this suit. It is contended by appellee that this amount was overpaid on the shipment first made on January 11th; that its manager, Pentecost, had no authority to make full payment on the first shipment; and that the excess charge for the conductor made by appellant was in violation of a written contract governing the price, which contract was entered into by both parties prior thereto and to which contract the Rural Electrification Association was also a party.

The lower Court, sitting as a jury, in refusing recovery to appellant, based its holding, in a short statement, on the ground that such a price contract was entered into on December 17, 1947, that appellant knew it was bound by it, and that both parties tried in vain to get the R.E.A. to change it.

(1,2) Conceding there was a written contract between the parties governing the price of materials, they still had a right to change that contract by mutual agreement. All of the evidence shows that the contract was changed in this instance by agreement, between appellant, on the one hand, and Pentecost, as manager of appellee, on the other hand. It is insisted by appellee, however, that Pentecost had no authority to agree to such a change. We see no merit in this contention. The well-established rule by which we must be guided here is briefly stated in *Chalmers & Son v. Bowen,* . . .from which opinion we quote:

A principal is not only bound by the acts of the agent done under express authority, but he is also bound by all acts of a general agent which are within the apparent scope of his authority, whether they have been authorized by the principal or not, and even if they are contrary to express directions. The principal in such case is not only bound by the authority actually given to the general agent, but by the authority which the third person dealing with him has a right to believe has been given to him.

(3) As we view the record there is no evidence to show that Pentecost was not acting "within the apparent scope of

his authority" when he agreed, on behalf of appellee, to the change in price, but there is abundant evidence to show he was so acting. Without encumbering this opinion by detailing the evidence, it is deemed sufficient to point out: that Pentecost had been the manager for several years, clothed with full apparent authority to transact business of this same character for appellee; he had formerly made similar purchases from appellant; he wrote checks on his company and none were turned down; and his transactions were only supervised by the board of directors meeting for an hour or two each month, at which time they scarcely, if ever, made any objections or even checked over his records.

(5) In addition to what we have already said, even if it were not clearly shown that Pentecost had apparent authority to bind appellee in this instance, we are convinced from the uncontradicted evidence that the sale was ratified both by the actions and the lack of action on the part of the board of directors. In this connection the evidence shows that at least one of the directors knew the terms and conditions of the transaction before shipment was made; that full payment by check signed by Pentecost and one director was made on January 20th; that the material was accepted by and used to the advantage of appellee; that the board of directors met (with Pentecost) and had opportunity to raise objections in February, March and April, but it failed to do so.

For the reasons stated and since there is no dispute over the amount in controversy, the judgment of the lower Court is reversed and remanded to the trial Court with directions to enter judgment in favor of appellant in the amount sued for.

In the final analysis, the apparent authority in this case stems from the title *general manager* and the fact that the party holding this title had in fact acted for several years as though he had the customary authority of a general manager.

The case may well have been decided in the same way if the party holding the title had not actually acted as manager for a long period of time. Though that evidence certainly helped, third parties would ordinarily be entitled to assume that even a newly appointed general manager would have the usual authority of a general manager in the particular trade or business involved.

✱ Although this case does not involve the hospitality industry, it illustrates a common situation that can arise in almost any segment of business or industry. This is where an executive, with the authority to make contracts, makes a contract and then moves on. Is his successor bound by his contract? The answer, as stressed before, is yes, assuming that the first executive really was within his authority, either real or apparent.

In such a situation, the better policy is to live up to the contract at the outset, rather than incurring the ill will and the costs of litigation that may ensue, particularly since the law is that the contract will be enforceable against the firm anyway.

Management Ideas: The Area of Authority to Contract

1. An organization of any size has to delegate authority. The scope of authority becomes smaller as one follows down the organizational structure or becomes larger as an employee is promoted to higher and higher positions. It is up to the superior to judge whether a subordinate will assume the necessary responsibility which goes with a certain level of authority.[1] Only authority can be delegated—not responsibility. The latter is an intrinsic human quality. The device with which to spell out the authority of a given job is obviously the job description. Make it clear in the job description how far you want real authority to go.

2. Do not limit a person's real authority below his apparent authority; you will be held responsible in any event. For example, a night watchman, wearing a dark suit with a shirt and tie, who sits at a desk in the lobby, might be looked upon by guests as the night manager and, as such, carries apparent authority; namely, that of a night manager. There are two possible ways to clear this situation. You either have the man wear a kind of uniform and a badge saying "Hotel Security," or you give him real authority and change his job description.

3. The cashier in a restaurant has apparent authority in deciding such a question as credit. Give her some real authority as well. You can limit real authority of your employees by, for example, restricting the cashier's credit authority to, say,

---

1. When the manager or owner allocates authority he has to expect occasional errors in judgment by subordinates. However, some delegation is necessary if he expects to build up loyalty and instill confidence and promote decision-making.

$20 per case; your cook's or purchasing agent's authority to contract for you to $50 per one supplier.

4. Not only should real authority be clearly spelled out in the job description, but also you should make the effort to explain to the person holding the job the extent of the authority and the dangers involved when exceeding this authority for the organization.

5. Explain the difference between apparent and real authority to employees. Some employees who do not have any authority, like to assume it. This is part of the nature of a human being. It is part of his motivational system; "shining" with apparent authority is required by his ego-need fulfillment. To use authority means to have information available. Quite often lower echelon employees lack information and, as such, are not able to use authority wisely.

6. If a department head becomes ill, the substitute, if not otherwise directed, assumes implied authority. Check him out in your mind; can he act intelligently as your agent?

7. Check into the possibility of insuring your organization against liability arising out of authority claims. One club insured all members of the board against liability.

CHAPTER 9

Aspects of Collection for Services Rendered

Introduction

IN AN EARLIER chapter, it was explained that inns are required, as a matter of law, to accept all well-comported applicants. Almost inevitably, inns will, on occasion, accept unwanted applicants and then later be faced with nonpayment by the unwanted guest. Foodservice operations and private clubs do not have quite the same problem because they are not required to accept all well-comported applicants. However, restaurants, in particular, do not look for ways to turn away trade, and probably accept almost all applicants as do inns. Consequently, they too may be faced with nonpayment.

This chapter will examine in more detail some of the legal aspects surrounding collection for services rendered. The following topics will be considered.

1. Collection through suit in contract
2. Criminal statutes on fraud against innkeepers
3. Innkeeper's lien
4. Special considerations relating to checks
5. Credit cards as a means of payment

Collection Through Suit in Contract

The point was made earlier in this book that the duty of an innkeeper to accept all well-comported applicants is based upon a common law duty, and that when a guest offers to let a room and the inn accepts that offer, a contract results. Of course if payment is made in advance, few problems will arise. However, if credit is extended either for the room itself or for room service and if payment is refused, problems ensue. We also noted earlier that when a guest makes a confirmed reservation and fails to appear, a breach of contract results. In this case, the inn owes the guest the obligation to try to rent the room to others, but if this cannot be done, the inn legally, if not practically, may collect its losses by a suit in contract.

The major barriers to suit in contract are two: (1) locating the defendant and (2) meeting the high expense of suit. These are practical, not legal, questions. Probably most people applying for credit or making reservations are willing to provide their address if asked. Professional criminals would have fake identification, but such professionals are likely to constitute a small portion of credit losses.

The costs of suit are, of course, high; a conventional suit in the traditional trial court will be feasible only when large sums are in issue. However, there are often alternatives.

Most communities presently have small claims courts of some sort where laymen litigate claims without attorneys. In many states a small claim may be initiated merely by mailing or personally delivering the legal papers to the defendant. These papers are often prepared by clerks of the court.

In other cases, the best alternative might be to forward the claim to a collection agency. Collection agencies typically charge 50 percent of the face amount of a claim; i.e., for a $100 claim they will pay the inn $50 and then only if they collect. However, 50 percent is better than nothing. Collection agencies are able to make a profit collecting bad debts because they are set up to mail out dunning notices and engage in other collection activities on a mass production basis. They maintain national contacts so that claims arising in one section of the country incurred by a party living in another section can be forwarded to the latter's home. Most important, bills owed by a defendant can be accumulated and a number of accounts sued on in one legal action. Thus, it becomes feasible to go to court to collect many small acounts.

Knowledge of the fact that there are remedies available to the hospitality industry that might be successful in collecting accounts provides some credibility to the manager who is attempting to secure payment of a bill. He is in a position to point out, should he choose, that if the guest refuses to pay, additional steps can and may be taken which could be unpleasant (such as appearing in court) and embarrassing (such as having judgment entered against him).

Mention was made in the first chapter of the fact that even after judgment, a defendant can refuse to pay. However, the recourse in that event is the seizure of the defendant's property and a public auction. Usually the latter steps are not necessary.

The Innkeeper's Lien

As emphasized before, the law requires the innkeeper to provide accommodations to all well-comported parties who apply and who can be accommodated. Recognizing the fact that this places a severe burden upon the innkeeper, the law compensates for it to some extent by granting the innkeeper a lien. A lien is a right to hold property of a guest as security against payment. If payment is refused despite the holding of the guest's property by the inn, ultimately the property may be sold and the bill owing the inn deducted from the proceeds.

The innkeeper's lien has its origin in common law, when the innkeeper had a right to hold practically any property brought into the inn by the guest. Some exceptions, almost too ludicrous to mention in the sense that such claims would be advanced at all, have been established. The innkeeper may not strip the clothes off a guest, particularly a female, as part of his lien, and he may not place a lien over the U.S. mail brought into the inn by a mailman. Most hospitality operations should be able to live with these limitations.

Although the common law recognized an exceedingly broad lien over the property brought into the inn by the guest, most states have enacted statutes defining the exact nature of the innkeeper's lien. In order to fully understand one's legal rights, it will be necessary to check with an attorney to find out what the details of the innkeeper's lien are in the state. However, there are certain fairly general aspects of the lien.

Almost all liens cover most charges likely to be engendered during a normal stay at an inn. Included would be room,

room service, restaurant service, phone bills, and any agreed charges for automobile storage. Many state statutes narrow the type of property that may be subject to the lien, the most frequent limitation being simply that the property must belong to the guest and cannot belong to others, even though in the guest's possession.

One of the main problems with the innkeeper's lien is the fact that although the innkeeper is free to seize the property of the nonpaying guest, he is not free to sell the property and pocket the proceeds. He is likely to find himself in legal trouble if he does. In order to sell the property he must apply to the court, and this process is likely to cost at least as much as the proceeds of the sale. Consequently, the main value of the lien in these days of high legal fees is as a bargaining wedge against the guest, and then only if something fairly valuable happens to be in the luggage. Needless to say, guests who enter an inn in the expectation of not paying, do not bring valuable property with their baggage. When they do not, the innkeeper's lien is useless.

Fraud Against Innkeepers

The general principle was established in chapter 1 of this text that failure or even refusal to pay a debt is not, strictly speaking, illegal and most certainly will not result in a jail sentence. Debtors' prisons have been out of fashion for many years.

However, there are certain forms of crime which have as one of their elements a failure to pay money owed. These crimes are described by such titles as *Obtaining Money Under False Pretenses, Criminal Fraud,* or that crime with which we are most interested herein, *Fraud Against Innkeeper.*

Fraud has been discussed as a basis for a suit in contract in chapter 6. The essence of fraud is an intentional misrepresentation leading to damages by the party to whom the misrepresentation was made and who relied upon it. Fraud, as discussed in that context, is merely a civil remedy that is a basis for bringing a suit for damages or avoiding a contract.

When parties with fraudulent intent receive services from inns or restaurants, a civil suit is usually no help to the innkeeper. In the first place, he is unlikely to locate such parties, and if he does, they are likely to have no visible assets. Nonetheless, the innkeeper does have the legal duty to accept all well-comported applicants.

For these reasons, almost all states have enacted criminal statutes making it a crime to defraud an innkeeper intentionally. It should be emphasized that these statutes never make mere inability to pay an inn or restaurant bill a crime. More is required. Basically what is required to find someone guilty under these statutes is, first and foremost, proof of an intent to defraud at the time the services (whether at an inn or a restaurant) were contracted for and some trick, deceit, or false pretenses intentionally used by the guest at that time. Obviously, it requires a good deal of proof to establish that a nonpaying guest never intended to pay and that he tricked the innkeeper into extending services.

Another act covered by most statutes dealing with crimes against innkeepers is the surreptitious removal of baggage. Such statutes are designed to preserve the hotelman's lien. The defect with such statutes is that in order to violate them, the guest must resort to some concealment or subterfuge. Leaving disguised as a cleaning lady while pushing out a hamper filled with one's luggage would violate this statute. Brazenly walking out past the desk clerk who was reading a newspaper would not.

To what extent need management be concerned about reporting such acts to the police? False imprisonment was discussed earlier in chapter 3, and it should be clear that merely reporting a suspected crime does not constitute false imprisonment. There is a tort, malicious prosecution, in which the essence is falsely instigating criminal prosecution against a party. However, in order to prove malicious prosecution, the plaintiff in such an action must show first that his accuser was malicious, that is, was bringing the action because of meanness or vengeance and second, must show that his accuser had no probable cause, that is, no reasonable basis for reporting him to the police. It is submitted that careful and conscientious managers will be able to show that they are not malicious and not lacking in probable cause when their fraudulent guests are reported as violating Crimes Against Innkeepers.

However, the presence of these crimes in the criminal code of most states does not solve the innkeeper's problems. Probably professional criminals are aware of the codes and of ways to make sure that they are not caught within the highly technical requirements. Amateurs may occasionally be prosecuted under these acts but probably other amateurs do not know about them, so that the deterrent effect may be slight. It is our impression that few successful prosecutions are brought under these acts, so, realistically, management should look to its own devices to seek protection against the nonpaying guest.

Crimes Involving Checks

The check is, of course, a convenient method of making payment. However, it is merely an order to a bank to pay someone cash. It is not itself cash. Consequently, there are means by which a worthless check may be tendered and sometimes accepted for payment. We will address ourselves briefly to this problem. We will not undertake to explain the entire, complex, detailed area of the law known as negotiable instruments. It appears to us that the amount of time and effort necessary for a thorough grasp of this subject might better be spent on other areas of study.

The bank on which the check is drawn, i.e., the party ordered to pay the face amount, is known as the drawee. The party to whom payment is ordered to be paid is the payee, and the party ordering the drawee to pay the payee (i.e., the depositor) is the drawer.

Bad checks can arise in several different ways, every one of which could result in loss to the person accepting the bad check.

A payroll, social security, or other form of check already made out to a payee (the party to whom payment is directed) may be stolen. Alcoholics and narcotics users are particularly prone to this form of theft. Then, the thief may forge the name of the payee. Whoever cashes the check will probably be out that sum of money. He can recover only from the party to whom he gave the money and that party will be difficult to locate.

A forger may simply secure a blank check and insert someone else's name or invent one as drawer (party ordering the bank to pay). The result to the party cashing it will be the same.

Forgery is a serious crime in every jurisdiction, but the fact that the forger may be prosecuted is small comfort to the party who cashed the check. In most instances, although the forger is liable, he no longer has the funds to make good the loss.

A more difficult situation arises when a party signs his own name to a check, has a bank account, but has insufficient funds to cover the loss. Treatment of this situation varies from state to state. Almost everyone has on one occasion or another written an overdraft. Accidentally doing so is usually not a crime, though many states consider it strong evidence of a crime. The question is intent. Was the party attempting to obtain money fraudulently, or was he merely careless in keeping his accounts? Many states consider failure to make the check good upon notification that it has not cleared to be evidence of intent to commit a crime; usually, evidence of a pattern of writing many such checks is admissible to prove crime. The reader can only check the law in his particular jurisdiction to see how his own state treats this problem. In the final analysis, what is or is not a crime is not so important to the hospitality operation as the steps to be taken to avoid bad checks.

CASE

BLYE v. GLOBE-WERNICKE REALTY CO. et al., (NEW YORK 1973) 347 NYS 2d 170

JASEN, JUDGE

In August, 1971, Judy Blye took up residence at the Van Rensselaer Hotel in Manhattan. In October of that year, she was locked out of her room for nonpayment of one week's hotel charges amounting to $60.60. Pursuant to the inn-keeper's lien law (Lien Law, ¶181[1]), the hotel summarily seized her personal property (valued by her at about $700) without notice and without an opportunity for a hearing. She was left with only the clothes she was wearing, her purse with some personal identification, and small change.

An action was then commenced seeking a declaratory judgment of the unconstitutionality of section 181 of the Lien Law, a permanent injunction and damages for mental distress. Special Term, 328, N.Y. S 2d 257, dismissed the action on the authority of Waters & Co. v. Gerard. . . and the Appellate Division unanimously affirmed. . . The appeal is before us as of right on constitutional grounds.

Plaintiff asks that we reconsider our holding in the *Gerard* case *(supra)*, wherein the predecessor of section 181 of the Lien Law was upheld against a due process challenge. We

---

1. " ¶181. Liens of hotel, apartment hotel, inn, boarding, rooming and lodging house keepers.—A keeper of a hotel, apartment hotel, inn, boarding house, rooming house or lodging house, except an emigrant lodging house, has a lien upon, while in possession, and may detain the baggage and other property brought upon his premises by a guest, boarder, roomer or lodger for the proper charges due from him, on account of his accommodation, board, room and lodging, and such extras as are furnished at his request. If the keeper of such hotel, apartment hotel, inn, boarding, rooming or lodging house knew that the property brought upon his premises was not, when brought, legally in possession of such guest, boarder, roomer or lodger, or had notice that such property was not then the property of such guest, boarder, roomer or lodger, a lien thereon does not exist. An apartment hotel within the meaning of this section includes a hotel wherein apartments are rented for fixed periods of time, either furnished or unfurnished, to the occupants of which the keeper of such hotel supplies food, if required. A guest of an apartment hotel, within the meaning of this section, includes each and every person who is a member of the family of the tenant of an apartment therein, and for whose support such tenant is legally liable."

are also urged to hold that section 181 is violative of the constitutional guarantees against unreasonable searches and seizures.

We conclude that section 181 of the Lien Law is irreconcilable with evolving concepts of due process and is unconstitutional. Insofar as *Gerard* holds to the contrary, it is overruled. On this view, we do not reach the search and seizure question.

Turning to the contention that this summary remedy denies due process, we note that plaintiff's property was not seized by a State official, but by private persons—i.e., hotel personnel, acting pursuant to State law. The threshold question is, therefore, whether the requisite "State action" is present.

[3,4] It is clear that private conduct will not invoke the constitutional guarantees of due process. But it is equally without doubt that in some circumstances, the actions of a private citizen can become the actions of the State for purposes of the due process clause. . . .For instance, State action, or action under color of State law, has been readily found in racial discrimination cases. . . .generally, Honan, Law and Social Change; The Dynamics of the "State Action" Doctrine, Comment, Current Developments in State Action and Equal Protection of the Law, 4 Gonzaga L. Rev. 233.) And in recent years, another theory of State action has emerged. It holds that the actions of private persons, when performing traditionally public functions, may be attributed to the State for purposes of the Fourteenth Amendment.

[5] In this State, the execution of a lien, be it a conventional security interest, a writ of attachment, or a judgment lien traditionally has been the function of the Sheriff. On this view, "State action" can be found in an innkeeper's execution on his own lien. Then, too, it cannot be gainsaid that innkeepers are possessed of certain powers by virtue of section 181 of the Lien Law. By that token, their actions are clothed with the authority of State law and their actions may be said to be those of the State for purposes of the due process clauses.

[6-10] Procedural due process requires notice and an opportunity for a hearing before the State may deprive a person of a possessory interest in his property. The protection is not limited to necessaries although the relative weight of

the property interest involved may be relevant to the form of notice and hearing required by due process. Nor does the availability of the right turn on the relative degree of permanence of the deprivation, nor may it be defeated by provision for recovery of the property. Only an extraordinary or truly unusual situation will justify postponing notice and opportunity for a hearing. Thus, for example, summary seizure may be permissible where necessary to secure an important governmental or general public interest or where the need for prompt action is paramount.

[11] It cannot be said that the statute before us serves such an important governmental or general public interest. As the Supreme Court noted in an analogous context "no more than private gain is directly at stake." And as this case well illustrates, summary seizure of a guest's property may deprive him of the sum of his possessions. Consequently, it may affect his ability to hold a job, making him a burden to family or friends, or perhaps even a public charge.

Practically speaking, it is difficult to perceive how this statute affords the innkeeper any real protection against the transient intent on absconding and defaulting on his bill. Rather, the statute falls hardest on people such as this plaintiff who work in the community and make their residence at a hotel or other like establishment. With respect to this class of persons at least, the extraordinary remedy of summary seizure is especially harsh, oppressive, and, it would seem unnecessary. Nor does this statute limit summary seizure to those extraordinary situations necessitating prompt action— e.g., to secure the creditor's interest in obtaining jurisdiction for purposes of bringing a nonpayment suit or in preventing the debtor from removing or concealing his property to prevent future execution on any judgment that might be obtained. The fact is that the statutory scheme does not contemplate the bringing of a nonpayment suit, nor any judicial determination, pre or post seizure, of the validity of the keeper's claim. The statute sweeps broadly and, as a matter of course, permits the unchecked summary seizure of a guest's property without regard to the validity of the particular claim and without regard to whether the particular guest is likely to remove or conceal himself and his property if given notice and opportunity for a hearing. In resolving the conflicting interests and in light of the feasible alternatives, we believe the guest's interest in possession and use of his property outweighs the innkeeper's interest in summarily seizing that property to secure the payment of charges.

Conditioning the innkeeper's lien with procedural due process safeguards will not destroy it or leave the keeper at the mercy of the defaulting guest. The keeper's right under the Lien Law to seize a defaulting guest's property and to sell it at public auction (and the State's power to confer that right) is not questioned. All that is necessary is that the fundamentals of due process be observed. This imports that, absent extraordinary circumstances, the guest be afforded notice and the *opportunity* to be heard before being deprived of the possession of his property.

Accordingly, the order of the Appellate Division should be reversed, without costs, and the innkeeper's lien declared unconstitutional.

FULD, C.J., and BURKE, JONES and WACHTLER, J.J., concur with JASEN, J.

✱ *Does this case constitute the death knell of the innkeeper's lien? It certainly is the end of that lien in New York State. Whether the remaining 49 states will follow this decision remains to be seen, but the reader is advised to keep abreast of developments on this subject. Your state may be next.*

CASE

THE PEOPLE OF THE STATE OF COLORADO
v.
AUSLEY (COLORADO 1974) 523 P 2d 460

HODGES, JUSTICE

The defendant, James D. Ausley, appeals from a conviction of the felony charge of procuring more than $50 in food or accommodations with the intent to defraud. Defendant asserts that the statute is unconstitutional for three reasons. We find no merit in the arguments and therefore affirm the conviction.

The defendant first argues that the statute under which he was convicted is unconstitutional because it denied to him equal protection of the laws. We do not agree.

The General Assembly has fixed the felony-misdemeanor dividing line at $100 for many crimes. For example, thefts of over $100 are a felony and a misdemeanor if under $100.

However, the dividing line between felonies and misdemeanors is $50 for procuring food or accommodations with intent to defraud.

"Any person who, with intent to defraud, procures food or accommodations in any public establishment, as defined in this article, without making payment therefor in accordance with his agreement with such public establishment, shall be guilty of a misdemeanor if the total amount due under such agreement shall be fifty dollars or less, and, upon conviction thereof, shall be punished by a fine of not more than five hundred dollars or by imprisonment in the county jail for not more than ninety days, or by both such fine and imprisonment; and, if the amount due under such agreement shall be more than fifty dollars, such person shall be guilty of a felony, and upon conviction thereof, shall be punished by imprisonment in the state penitentiary for a term of not less than one nor more than ten years."

The defendant argues there is no rational reason for convicting him of a felony for defrauding an innkeeper of $54 whereas he would have been convicted of only a misdemeanor had he taken $54 worth of groceries from a store without paying for them.

[1,2] We have repeatedly held that a statute is presumed to be constitutional, and the one attacking its validity has the burden of establishing its unconstitutionality beyond a reasonable doubt. We have further held that "if any state of facts can reasonably be conceived that will justify the classification, the existence of these facts will be assumed by the courts in order to uphold the legislation."

[3] In upholding the classification, the trial court stated that the dividing line was set at $50 because the usual motel bill for one night is under $50. The legislature may have deemed the crime more serious if more than $50 was defrauded, since such a bill generally would involve more than

one night of food or accommodation, and thus, would involve a series of offenses extending over a period of more than one day. We hold that this is a rational reason for the difference in treatment. People v. McKenzie, *supra.*

II

[4] The defendant next argues that the statute is unconstitutional because it makes failure to pay a contractual debt a crime in violation of Colo. Const. Art. II, Sec. 12.

The defendant argues that the prosecution would only have to introduce evidence that the defendant was indebted to the innkeeper, that the bill was not paid, and then rest. The intent to defraud would then be inferred from the nonpayment of debt.

In People v. Vinnola, relied heavily upon by the defendant, we held the short check statute unconstitutional because that statute lacked fradulent intent as an element. The statute in *Vinnola* is clearly distinguishable from the statute involved in this case. Here, the statute specifically requires the intent to defraud. Such an intent could not be inferred solely from the naked fact of nonpayment as argued by the defendant.

III

[5] The defendant asserts that the statute denies equal protection because it makes the prosecution of the crime dependent upon the willingness of the innkeeper to accept late payment.

In People v. Vinnola, *supra*, the statute involved specifically provided that it would be a complete defense if the amount of the check was tendered within fifteen days after dishonor. We held that this provision unconstitutionally gives a third person control over whether or not a bad check passer is convicted. The holder of the check could say he would not file a complaint if he received his money within fifteen days. The statute in the instant case contains no such provision.

Judgment affirmed.

DAY, J., dissents.

ERICKSON, J., does not participate.

✱ *This case merely establishes the fact that despite all we have said, it is possible to secure convictions under the Fraud Against Innkeepers Acts. Possibly we underestimate the deterrent effect such statutes might have if vigorously enforced.*

Management Ideas: Personal and Travelers Checks

PERSONAL CHECKS

1. Set up, in writing, a clear procedure for accepting checks. This procedure should include total limits, cash limits, identification, stamping requirements ("For Deposit Only"), authorization, and calling the guest's bank to see if the guest is known to the bank. Then, communicate the procedure to your employees. New employees present a higher risk than present employees because the former do not want to be labeled "inefficient" or "slow" and are also more easily intimidated by guests.

2. Insist on identifications with photographs (although even those can be forged).

3. Do not accept postdated, third-party checks, checks drawn on an out-of-town bank, or checks from a minor.

4. Limit the amount of the check to the amount owed.

5. You may want to consider taking a snapshot of and/or a fingerprint (with a "no-color" ink) of the guest.

6. Consider subscribing to a bad check notification service.

7. On each check have a stamp placed by the cashier or assistant manager as a reminder to verify date, room number, amount, and identification taken at the time the check is accepted, as illustrated below.

DATE	
ROOM NO.	
AMT.	
ID.	
INITIAL	

8. If in doubt, do not accept any check. The innkeeper must accept nearly anyone, but he has no duty to extend credit.

TRAVELERS CHECKS

When handling travelers checks, the counter-signing of the check in full view of the cashier constitutes the whole security system. Therefore:

1. Watch for a light tracing of the original signature in the place where the counter-signature will go. Felt pens will cover the tracing, but a ball-point pen will not.

2. Have the guest sign the travelers check in the cashier's full view—not covered by one hand.

3. Watch for the guest who carries his writing hand in a sling— he might use it as an excuse to not correctly counter-sign the check.

4. If the cashier is uncertain about a counter-signature, have the guest repeat the signature on the blank back of the check.

5. Do not let the cashier be hurried, pressured, or confused by the guest—it might be a technique.

Management Ideas: Credit Cards

1. Set up clear procedures for handling credit card sales, including ideas discussed below, and communicate these ideas to employees.

2. Watch for credit cards that have expired, are not yet valid, or have been altered.

3. Check the issuer's cancellation list. The operation that has received notice of cancellation and extends credit on the cancelled credit card can be held liable for the ensuing debt.

4. Compare the signature on the credit card with that on the sales slip.

5. Compare the type of credit card with the attire of the person. Does he fit? Admittedly in these times of casual dress, this is not foolproof.

6. Do not accept credit cards from minors.

7. Do not allow yourself or the cashier to be rushed in carrying out your procedures with credit cards.

Management Ideas: Innkeeper's Lien

There is only one bit of advice which can be given: do not try to hold the guest's luggage. It is not worth the trouble. The emphasis has to be on prevention. Several suggestions were made earlier in regard to collecting a guest's bill.

CHAPTER 10

The Administrative Agency

Introduction

MOST OF THE LEGAL situations that we have discussed up to this point have involved cases derived from the common law of the various states, that is, the court's decision was usually based upon previous decisions, and these decisions were ultimately traceable back to the English common law. Occasionally, a state statute changed or modified the common law of the state, but usually no statutes at all came into play.

The remainder of this text involves a radically different form of law. First, the remaining chapters deal primarily with federal law rather than state law. Congress, of course, is authorized to act when the subject matter of legislation affects interstate commerce.

Second, these bodies of law are made up almost entirely of legislation. Instead of merely amending common law rule, Congress drafted the legislative programs considered in the next three chapters. The only non-legislative component in this Congress-made law is that now and then a judicial interpretation may have sharpened or modified the meaning of the legislation.

Third, and finally, these bodies of law are all administered by administrative agencies. Because the reader might not be familiar with the nature and operation of administrative agencies, we will undertake to provide a brief explanation of these peculiar organs of our government.

Nature of the Administrative Agency

Administrative agencies may be created at the federal, state, or local level though, as already stated, the ones we will discuss are federal. When a legislative body designs a complex new program that would be difficult and complicated to enforce through existing bodies such as the police, the legislature usually creates a new body with enforcement powers. Often, the complexity and detail of the new program is so great that the legislature delegates to the new body the power to write in the details of the law. And, the legislature may well delegate the judicial power to subpoena suspected violators and hold hearings to determine guilt or innocence.

In summary, the administrative agency created by Congress may well hold the usual executive power of providing day-to-day administration of some complex program, the legislative power of writing the detailed rules and regulations for the program, and the judicial power of conducting hearings to determine whether the rules and regulations have been violated.

The reason that legislative bodies create and delegate to administrative agencies is simply that legislators could not possibly cope with the detail necessary to administer many of our regulatory programs. Moreover, the legislators would not have the expert knowledge required, nor the time.

Examples of federal regulatory agencies are the Security Exchange Commission, which regulates the security markets; the Interstate Commerce Commission, which regulates land transportation; the Civil Aeronautics Board, which regulates airlines, and the Federal Trade Commission, which regulates unfair trade practices. In the following chapters we will look at the National Labor Relations Board, which regulates labor-management relations; the Equal Employment Opportunity Commission, which attempts to ensure equal opportunity in employment, and the Occupational Safety and Health Administration, which supervises health and safety conditions in the employment situation.

Operation of Administrative Agency

Each of these agencies has field men who look into questionable situations relating to employment and who can initiate a complaint. If there is a complaint, each agency has the power to conduct a hearing which determines, in effect, whether or not the complaint was justified. In each case there is some provision for seeking review by a federal court. However, review is of only limited scope; the facts, that is, what actually happened in some dispute, are normally left to the agency to determine and are ordinarily not subject to review. The main function of the court is to make sure that interpretation of the law as made by the agency is correct.

Obviously, the attitude and the decisions of these administrative agencies have an enormous effect upon the industries they regulate. It is imperative not only that management keep in touch with the direction of these attitudes and decisions, but also that appropriate trade groups continue to maintain contact so that their interests, problems, and point of view may be explained.

CHAPTER 11

Labor Management Relations

Introduction

THERE ARE TWO distinct sets of problems in the area of labor management relations. First, there is the practical problem of keeping the work force sufficiently happy with wages, hours, working conditions, and fringe benefits so that they will be well-motivated employees, or, if not, will at least not go out on strike. This set of problems may be dealt with by common sense or, at a more sophisticated level, by personnel managers or industrial psychologists. However, though they are certainly important, these problems are beyond the scope of this text.

Second, there is the legal problem of complying with extensive state and federal law concerned with labor management relations. This law is complex. To some employers it seems to restrict unduly what were thought to be management prerogatives. The fact of the matter is that the present law of labor management relations places definite limits on the right of management to fire or discipline employees, at least for acts relating to union activities.

Although it has not always been the case, at the present time the right of employees to join or organize themselves into a union is protected by federal law and by the law of most states. We state this fact at the outset because most of what follows is an elaboration upon this basic premise. An employer who attempts to block formation of a union or to discourage his employees from joining one is courting serious legal consequences, and an employer who has the intention of doing so might as well consult a labor attorney at the outset, because he is certain to require extensive advice.

While both federal and state law regulate labor relations, in the event of any conflict between the two the federal law will govern. Moreover most state law is patterned after the federal law. It is impossible to even consider details of state law because of the large number of state systems involved. For these reasons, the discussion below is confined to the federal sphere.

Federal law is confined in its application to firms engaged in interstate commerce, but the definition of interstate commerce is very broad, and many, if not most, hospitality firms would fall within the definition.

The federal labor management relations law is administered by an administrative agency, the National Labor Relations Board, hereafter abbreviated NLRB. This board, supported by the usual administrative machinery, consists of five members. If a serious question arises as to whether either labor or management is in violation of the law administered by the NLRB, the agency will conduct an investigation and may conduct hearings before a trial examiner to determine if a violation has occurred.

Certification

Usually, the first stage on the road to full collective bargaining between labor and management is the certification of a bargaining unit. The employees are entitled to request an NLRB supervised election for the purpose of determining their bargaining unit at any time that 30 percent of the employees indicate their approval of any such unit. Usually, of course, the bargaining unit approved will be an existing union, but it could be a locally formed union or even an individual.

If more than one bargaining unit has support—usually rival unions—these two, or even more, will be placed on the ballot.

There are a number of very technical and difficult questions relating to the issue of what is the appropriate bargaining group. Should each craft or trade in a plant be represented individually, or should all belong to the same unit? Should the units go beyond the plant into other plants under the same management? These questions are too complex to resolve here, but management should at least be aware that there can be significant questions as to the number and nature of the bargaining units.

Once a unit is certified for bargaining purposes, it becomes the legal duty of management to bargain collectively with that unit. Management must somehow live with that unit unless at some time it appears that the unit no longer carries majority support. Should this happen, another election can be called by either management or labor for the purpose of decertifying the bargaining representative.

Much of the activity of the NLRB is involved in investigating and prosecuting unfair labor practices by management or labor. What constitutes an unfair labor practice is defined by statute. There is one list of unfair practices applicable to management and another list applicable to labor.

Unfair Practices: Management

The first act forbidden to management is interference with the rights of labor to engage in union activities. Such interference might include interrogation of employees, surveillance, threats or promises, changes in terms of employment, attempts to influence the outcome of an election, sponsorship of anti-union petitions, and otherwise discouraging union activity.

Management is restricted, though not completely forbidden, from making anti-union speeches. Management is forbidden to make such speeches on company premises and during working time less than 24 hours before the certification election. Even before this deadline, the management must provide equal opportunity for labor to give its side.

Restriction of union activities must be handled with care. Essentially, management has a right to forbid activities that would interfere with normal work during working hours, but they cannot prevent discussion between employees, and they cannot prevent union activities (often distributing literature or circulating petitions) on the employees' own time, such as lunch hours.

Management must avoid any attempt to influence any union or bargaining agent. Sheer generosity by management is outlawed, on the theory that if management donates money to the union, the union may become more responsive to management than to labor. In short, the day of the company union is over.

Any discrimination against employees in their jobs or working conditions is an unfair practice if related to either encouraging or discouraging union membership. A number of cases have held that union members were improperly fired even when they engaged in outrageous acts such as drinking on the job. The common denominator in these cases is that management did nothing in the way of discipline until the employee's union activities became an irritant, thus suggesting that the employee was disciplined for union activity rather than for bad conduct.

Finally, it is an unfair labor practice for either management or labor to refuse to bargain collectively, in good faith, should a dispute arise.

There is no obligation on the part of management to yield to demands relating to such questions as wages, hours, and working conditions, assuming management is not in violation of some law such as the Minimum Wage Law or Occupational Safety and Health Act. However, both sides must bargain in good faith. To some extent, the notion of good faith is a matter of common sense and presupposes a course of dealing whereby the parties agree to show up at the agreed meetings, consider the opposite proposals, and make counter proposals of their own and, in general, conduct themselves in a manner suggesting an honest desire to bring negotiations to an agreed conclusion. In a situation in which the parties are at a complete impasse, whether each is bargaining in good faith or not can be a difficult question, but by that time management would have hired legal counsel anyway; for this reason, the issue need not be discussed exhaustively in this brief treatment.

Union representatives are guaranteed by law the right to present grievances on behalf of the union or of union members to management. Once a collective bargaining agreement between management and labor is signed, it will usually contain a detailed grievance procedure in which low level union representatives, termed shop stewards, are authorized to present minor grievances to the foremen, who are the low level management representatives. If a solution is not possible at the lower levels of responsibility, the grievances will be referred to progressively higher levels.

It should be mentioned that while management is not legally obligated to agree to particular demands relating to wages, hours, and working conditions, once management has agreed to aspects of these demands in the collective bargaining agreement, violation of the agreed terms may be an unfair labor practice, with serious consequences for the firm.

Unfair Practices: Labor

Aside from refusing to bargain collectively, it is also an unfair practice on the part of labor to restrain or coerce employees in the exercise of their rights. Usually, this consists of attempting to coerce employees into joining a union or, conceivably, into not joining a union. In any event, aside from mere persuasion, labor has no right to influence or attempt to influence decisions of any members of the work force on any question relating to representation or collective bargaining.

Moreover, labor is forbidden from causing, or attempting to cause, the employer to discriminate against any employee. The usual pattern in which this question might become an issue is when the union attempts to pressure management into hiring only union members, firing non-union members (unless the state involved permits a closed shop, in which case this is legal), or discriminating against one union in favor of another.

The secondary boycott is illegal. A secondary boycott arises when a union is displeased with firm "A," and firm "A" has extensive dealings with firm "B." The union strikes or boycotts firm "B," with the message that it had better quit dealing with firm "A." The unfairness to "B" is obvious, which is why this practice has been declared an unfair labor practice.

When one union is certified by the NLRB, labor has no right to even attempt to force management to recognize another union. To do so is to commit an unfair labor practice. Obviously, the proper route for labor, if it is dissatisfied with its bargaining representative, is to petition the NLRB for another election.

Jurisdictional disputes constitute an unfair labor practice.

The jurisdictional dispute arises when one union becomes involved in a struggle with another union, usually over assignment of jobs. Sometimes both unions threaten to strike if they do not get their way. Obviously, this puts management in an impossible position.

Three other unfair labor practices need hardly be commented upon. Excessive initiation fees for new members of unions are unfair, but there have been very few cases in recent years involving this question. Featherbedding, that is, creating jobs where there is really nothing to do, is unfair, but this provision has not been enforced with much consistency. Finally, mass picketing, that is, picketing in such force that the effect is to intimidate people who might cross the line rather than to merely inform them of a dispute, is, with good reason, an unfair practice.

Economic Pressure

Despite extensive regulation by the NLRB, labor and management continue to have the right to do battle if they wish. Labor is guaranteed the right to strike.

Just as labor may strike in order to put economic pressure on management, so may management conduct a lock-out, that is, shut down operations to put economic pressure on labor.

Naturally, harmonious labor-management relations are usually desirable. However, there may be instances in which demands by labor are so excessive that they may not be worth the price. When this appears to be the case, probably it is worthwhile to call in professional labor-management relations advisors.

Management Ideas: Labor-Management Relations

Despite the limitations of a short discussion of this type, some of the following points will be helpful to the hospitality manager.

1. Management cannot interfere with elections for certifying which union will be the bargaining unit or with other union elections through coercion, threats, interrogating employees, discharging or temporarily laying off employees, granting benefits, or any other act that would appear to reward or punish employees.

2. However, there are activities which management can engage in without violating the Labor-Management Relations Act. If it refrains from expressions containing any threat of reprisal or promise of benefit, management can express any views, arguments, or opinion in written, printed, graphic, or visual form. Messages can be sent to employees or put up on bulletin boards. In addition, employees may be addressed orally up to 24 hours before the election polls are opened, so long as the address is non-coercive.

3. Management may question employees concerning union activities as long as it does not interfere with the employees' protected rights and as long as no threats or promises of benefits are made.

4. Management cannot dominate or interfere with the formation or administration of any labor organization, nor may it contribute financial or other support to such an organization.

5. If the majority of the employees stage a walk-out from the hospitality operation's business because of extremely uncomfortable working conditions, they may be within the law, regardless of whether they belong to a union or not.

6. Management cannot discharge an employee because of his union activities. Do not use pretexts to justify discharge. The following reasons have, on special occasions, been held to constitute pretexts and ruled illegal: insubordination, disobeying instructions, drunkenness, calling a supervisor an obscene name, being absent from work without permission, physical inability to do the work, and absenteeism. This is not to say that any of the grounds above might not be sufficient to discharge an employee. However, when the real reason for discharge appears to be union activity, the administrators of the NLRB will be skeptical about charges of misconduct.

7. Management does not have an absolute right to close its inn or restaurant and go out of business. This may be done only if it is for economic reasons and is in no way connected with present or future labor disputes or union activities.

8. In case of an economic strike, i.e., one which is called solely for the purpose of enforcing demands for improved wages, hours, and other terms and conditions of employment, management cannot hire temporary replacements (strikebreakers) but can hire permanent replacements. In the case of a strike protesting unfair labor practice, strikers cannot be replaced either by temporary or permanent replacements. However, management can hire temporary replacements during an economic strike if the union fails to notify management of intent to strike sixty days prior to the contract expiration or modification date.

9. Strikers engaging in an economic strike may nonetheless be discharged if they engage in violence or misconduct, mass picketing, or attempted prevention of guests or suppliers from entering the inn or restaurant.

10. The union may not force management to designate some particular executive favored by the union as the management bargaining representative. Management is entitled to negotiate through an attorney should it wish.

11. The union must give management reasonable time to consult with the management bargaining representative before calling an economic strike.

12. Agreements whereby management agrees to a "preferential hiring agreement," which gives preference in hiring to union members, are illegal. However, a union shop, which requires everyone employed to join the union, is legal in many states.

13. It is good management practice to assume that there is cause for a grievance before making a judgment. An investigation should be conducted with an open mind. This is especially important today in matters of employees' safety and health in light of recent Occupational Safety and Health Act legislation.

14. Whether management is dealing with a union or not, certain procedures should be followed in disciplinary actions. Effective personnel practice requires that management establish a list of rules of conduct. The list should clearly specify the particular disciplinary action which will result from each violation of a rule. Any violation should be followed by a written warning giving the details and requiring the signature of the employee. One copy should remain with the employee, the original with the personnel office. This type of record will substantiate any discharge. There should be a grace period after which certain violations become void. Otherwise, some operations might find themselves with no employees.

15. Management is required to bargain collectively with the representative of a majority of its employees (if there is a representative), even if no union is involved.

16. Groups of managerial employees need not be recognized as a bargaining unit. Managerial employees are those who formulate, determine, and carry out management policies. Management trainees who are college graduates may well fall into the same category.

17. Since the hospitality operation is responsible for its managerial employees, make certain that they understand how to handle the different forms of labor problems that are frequently encountered.

CHAPTER 12

Equal Opportunity in Employment

Introduction

THERE IS A vast and developing body of law designed to en-sure that employees are treated equally. Broadly speaking this body of law is designed to ensure that employers do not discriminate against one person in favor of another on the basis of race, color, religion, sex, national origin, or age.[1] Even though some of the Constitutional provisions or federal stat-utes central to this set of laws are fairly old, the current em-phasis on assuring equal opportunity in employment is a rather recent development, and the law is somewhat confus-ing. In this area, conflicting decisions between different courts are not unusual, and instances of a court departing from its own prior decisions are not unheard of.

Another source of difficulty is simply the abundance of

---

1. At the federal level, all of these except age discrimination are administered by the Equal Employment Opportunity Commission. Age discrimination is adminis-tered by the Dept. of Labor. However, its approach to problems is similar to EEOC.

legal authority involved. The federal law on this subject includes provisions of the U. S. Constitution and a number of more or less interlocking federal statutes, as well as rules and decisions produced by a federal administrative agency, the Equal Employment Opportunity Commission (usually abbreviated EEOC).

Most states also have their own state constitutional provisions bearing on the question of equal opportunity. Many have state legislation which usually is enforced through a state administrative agency, and many cities have local ordinances enforced by a local administrative agency concerned with the problem of equality in employment.

Because of the multitude of sources which contribute to the law of equal employment opportunity, we do not feel that it is feasible in a brief treatment to explore in detail the provisions of each federal statute or constitutional mandate, much less the various state and local provisions. Instead, we will concentrate on the sorts of acts by employers that are usually found to be illegal. Regardless of whether the law, or the agency enforcing the law, is at the federal, state, or local level, there is a fair degree of unanimity between the agencies holding that certain types of practice are illegal. This, therefore, is the area we will emphasize.

Before turning to a detailed examination of some of the acts held to be illegal, one thing ought to be noted. Although the basic rule is simply that there be no discrimination based upon race, color, religion, sex, national origin, or age, this basic rule is not so easy to follow. As will be seen below, violations have been found in circumstances in which many reasonable people would not have believed that discrimination was present. Intent is not required to find an equal opportunity violation, and probably many significant cases have occurred as a result of oversight rather than through any desire to discriminate. Some decisions rendered under these laws will seem strange to many readers. On the other hand, the need for some legal assistance to various minorities in securing employment can hardly be doubted after examining data concerning the differential in unemployment rates and yearly income between minority groups and native-born, middle-aged white males.

Finally, whatever else may be said about this area of the law, it is certainly important. Findings of past discrimination often carry with them a court order that back pay be awarded to the parties discriminated against. When these groups consist of large numbers of employees, the awards can be immense. A settlement of $20 million was arranged against American Telephone and Telegraph, $14 million against Ford Motor, and an award against several airlines may also reach those figures.

What Does the Law Say?

The law of equal opportunity forbids discrimination on the basis or race, color, religion, sex, national origin, or age. The above listing places these categories of discrimination in their order of importance as a source of litigation. In other words, more suits are brought on the basis of sex discrimination, with race next in importance, and so on.

One authority in the area of equal employment commented that there are so many prohibitions in effect which outlaw discrimination that nowadays one has to be suicidal to discriminate deliberately. However, intent to discriminate is not necessary to a finding that one is practicing discrimination, and the path is strewn with traps for the unwary. Almost any practice that results in disfavoring any of the protected minorities may well result in a finding that the employer is practicing discrimination. The main exception is that if valid, scientific data can be produced to demonstrate that the alleged discriminatory practice is, in fact, a valid means of selecting personnel for a particular job, the practice may be successfully defended.

For example, educational requirements consistently discriminate against racial minorities, who tend to be less well educated. Therefore, educational requirements may well be held to be discriminatory unless it can be shown that the level of education required is a necessity for the particular job in mind. For example, do the service personnel of a restaurant need to have completed a high school education?

A certain level of proficiency on some standardized tests is required. Again, most tests do, in fact, discriminate in favor of the dominant majority; hence, unless the material tested upon can be shown to be related to job performance, use of the tests is likely to be held to be discrimination. An appropriate arithmetic test given to the above service personnel might be in order, if the personnel are required to add guest checks. It would be discriminatory to present the same test to the housekeeping personnel. These and additional examples of unintentional discrimination will be explored below, but the point bears repeating. Any factor which appears to screen out protected minority groups from employment or promotion is suspect, and management must be alert in recognizing such factors and correcting them.

Recruitment

The first step in the employment process is recruitment. Steps should be taken to assure that all the protected groups have equal access to job information, so that the charge may not be made that discrimination occurs because some groups never hear of the availability of jobs. Advertisements must, of course, never make reference to race, color, religion, sex, national origin, or age. An advertisement stating, "Salesman wanted," was held discriminatory against women by a local anti-discrimination agency. Evidently the ad should have read "Salesperson wanted." Here are two actual examples.

Of the two ads, one seems to fulfill the requirements, the one seeking a district manager with the adjunct, "An Equal Opportunity Employer m/f." If an employer hires largely through a union hiring hall, both employer and union may be in legal difficulty if union practices foster discrimination.

There are a few instances where discrimination has been held justified by economic exigencies, but these are so rare as to be beside the point. It has been held that cocktail lounges may confine their hiring to attractive female cocktail waitresses, on the ground that a seductive atmosphere is a business necessity for a successful operation. Possibly on the theory that the atmosphere might be too seductive, massage parlors have been held to local ordinances that only males may be employed to massage other males. Chinese and other specialty restaurants have been permitted to confine their employment to persons of the appropriate national origin. No doubt, age requirements are valid qualifications for some types of employment, but the burden will be on management to produce objective evidence that persons above a certain age ordinarily cannot perform the duties involved.

The Bona Fide Occupational Qualification

The exception noted above (hiring only females as cock-tail waitresses) along with other exceptions to the general rule, have been validated through establishing a "bona fide occupational qualification," abbreviated BFOQ. If it can be established that only a certain class, such as men or women, can satisfactorily perform a certain job, a BFOQ exception can be established. However, the burden of proof is upon the employer claiming a BFOQ. Employment qualification based primarily on tradition or past employment history is exactly what the Equal Employment Opportunity Laws are designed to combat and cannot be relied upon to establish a BFOQ. Often employers assume that a valid distinction exists (such as barring women from jobs requiring some lifting), which cannot be proved when put to the test.

Applications

The next step in employment often consists of the applicant filling out a form provided by the prospective employer. All employers should carefully examine the forms they are using if they have not already done so, with an eye toward eliminating any questions that might prove troublesome later. The basic question for the employer to ask about his form is this: does the form ask any questions that the employer cannot justify as being necessary for making a rational decision as to hiring the applicant? If so, the employer may well be in trouble.

For example, a question as to race or religion is almost bound to be irrelevant, so we will not dwell on this. The same is true as to sex, because there is almost no job that, at least from the legal point of view, cannot be performed by women. Does the form ask if the applicant is married? If so, this may suggest discrimination against married women, which is not permissible. Does it ask for height and weight? Such questions have been held discriminatory against Orientals, Mexicans, and women, except in those very rare cases where objective evidence specifically shows that minimum height and weight requirements are necessary to job performance. Age, as noted above, is ordinarily irrelevant unless the contrary can be shown. The same is frequently true as to education. The danger of having irrelevant questions on the application form is simply that chance variables may have eliminated many of some group without any intent to discriminate. However, if statistics show some minority group to be at a disadvantage in securing jobs and if membership in such a group is determined from the job application, it is much more difficult for the employer to prove his assertion that the result was indeed owing to chance.

TABLE 8

EMPLOYMENT APPLICATION

DATE _____

PERSONAL INFORMATION

NAME _____ TELEPHONE NO. _____ SOCIAL SECURITY NO. _____

PRESENT ADDRESS _____ LENGTH OF RESIDENCE _____

PREVIOUS ADDRESS _____ LENGTH OF RESIDENCE _____

DATE OF BIRTH _____ (1) SEX ___ M ___ F ___ HEIGHT _____ WEIGHT _____

MARITAL STATUS _____ NAME OF SPOUSE _____ CITIZEN? _____ NO. OF DEPENDENTS _____

(2) CHILDREN (List Names & Birthdates) _____

EMPLOYMENT INFORMATION

POSITION DESIRED _____ DATE YOU CAN START _____ SALARY DESIRED _____

REFERRED BY _____ DO YOU DESIRE? FULL TIME _____ PART TIME _____ PERMANENT _____ TEMPORARY _____

APPLIED TO _____/EMPLOYED BY _____ A DOUBLETREE BEFORE? _____ WHEN _____ WHERE _____

LIST ANY FRIENDS/RELATIVES PRESENTLY EMPLOYED BY DOUBLETREE _____

DO YOU OWN YOUR HOME? _____ RENT? _____ DO YOU OWN A CAR? _____ MILES/TIME TO DOUBLETREE _____

EDUCATION/MILITARY

TYPE OF SCHOOL	NAME/LOCATION OF SCHOOL	YEARS ATTENDED	MAJOR	YEAR GRADUATED/ DEGREE
GRAMMAR				
HIGH SCHOOL				

(cont.)

TABLE 8 (cont.)

COLLEGE		
TRADE, BUSINESS, CORRESPONDENCE		

ARE YOU PRESENTLY STUDYING? _____ SCHOOL _____ SUBJECTS _____

FOREIGN LANGUAGES YOU SPEAK FLUENTLY _____ READ _____ WRITE _____

WHAT OFFICE MACHINES CAN YOU OPERATE? _____

MILITARY EXPERIENCE? _____ DRAFT STATUS _____ LOTTERY NO. _____

WORK EXPERIENCE

DATE (MONTH & YEAR)	NAME/ADDRESS OF EMPLOYER	SALARY	POSITION	SUP.	REASON FOR LEAVING
FROM					
TO					
FROM					
TO					
FROM					
TO					
FROM					
TO					
FROM					
TO					

LOFTIN'S PHOENIX 254-6611

MISCELLANEOUS

③ HAVE YOU EVER BEEN ARRESTED? _____ FOR WHAT? _____ CAN YOU BE BONDED? _____

④ HAVE YOU EVER FILED FOR WORKMEN'S COMPENSATION? _____ WHEN? _____ WHAT FOR? _____

⑤ HAVE YOU EVER FILED FOR UNEMPLOYMENT COMPENSATION? _____ WHEN? _____

⑥ HAS YOU DRIVER'S LICENSE EVER BEEN REVOKED? _____

⑦ HAVE YOU USED ALCOHOL OR NARCOTICS TO EXCESS? _____

REFERENCES

NAME	ADDRESS	BUSINESS	YEARS ACQUAINTED

PHYSICAL RECORD

LIST ANY PHYSICAL DEFECTS/HANDICAPS: HEARING _____ VISION _____ SPEECH _____ OTHER _____

LIST ANY SERIOUS ILLNESSES/OPERATIONS/ACCIDENTS AND APPROXIMATE DATE _____

IN CASE OF EMERGENCY, PLEASE NOTIFY _____ TELEPHONE NO. _____

(cont.)

TABLE 8 (cont.)

I certify that this information is accurate and complete. I understand that misrepresentation or omission of facts called for is cause for dismissal.

SIGNATURE _____ DATE _____

DO NOT WRITE BELOW THIS LINE

INTERVIEWED BY _____ DATE _____

	EXCELLENT	GOOD	AVERAGE	POOR
PERSONALITY	___	___	___	___
EXPERIENCE	___	___	___	___
ATTITUDE	___	___	___	___
APPEARANCE	___	___	___	___

REMARKS: _____

_____

_____

HIRED BY _____ DATE HIRED _____ STARTING DATE _____

DEPARTMENT _____ POSITION _____ SALARY _____ MANAGER'S SIGNATURE

There are certain questions in this employment application which either violate the law or are highly questionable and may be difficult to defend later. They include:

1. Sex, perhaps allowed only when you are looking for a cocktail waitress.
2. Marital status.
3. Have you ever been arrested?
4. Have you ever filed for workmen's compensation?
5. Have you ever filed for unemployment compensation?
6. Has your driver's license ever been revoked?
7. Have you used alcohol or narcotics to excess?

We would suggest that one eliminate the question "Can you be bonded?" and instead explain verbally that employment (e.g., as cashier) is contingent upon the employee's qualifying for bonding.

Some other questions, while not in violation of the law, are totally irrelevant and should also be reviewed, e.g., "Do you own your own home?" or "previous salary?" Always ask yourself, what is the relevance of the question to the job the applicant is applying for?

Job Skills

The next question is, what job skills can be required, and the answer, essentially, is no more than are reasonably necessary to satisfactory performance of the job. As stated above, the burden is upon the employer to explain his criterion, if it appears to discriminate against certain groups. This reasoning applies to education, height and weight, and specific attributes such as dexterity or strength. Usually a careful analysis of the skills necessary to every job must be made, and, if tests are employed, it must be shown that the tests indeed test accurately the possession by the applicant of these skills. This process is known as test validation and can only be accomplished by a person professionally trained in the arcane science of test validation.

Other Criteria

Certain other screening criteria are sometimes used, to the later sorrow of the employer. Arrest records, even when extensive, have been held not a valid basis for refusing employment, on the theory that some minorities are more subject to being arrested than the white majority; hence, the criterion of arrest records is discriminatory. Conviction, as distinguished from mere arrest, continues to be a valid basis for rejection.

Lack of separate toilet facilities for the two sexes has been held not a valid basis for excluding women. Long hair as a basis for rejection of men is an area subject to conflicting decisions, the usual arguments being that long hair violates health standards or alienates customers but, in response, the arguments that such factors have not inhibited the employment of women have often been found convincing. An employer who feels strongly about long-haired men should consult a lawyer, in order to find out what rule of law has been accepted in his jurisdiction, before using this as a basis for rejection.

Many states have special protective legislation applicable to women, which prevents their working more than a certain number of hours per day or week, or prevents them from working after certain hours in the evening. A number of such statutes have been reviewed by the courts recently, with the almost invariable result being that the statute was declared invalid because it violated federal constitutional or EEOC provisions. However, such a law presents the employer with a cruel dilemma. If he violates the law, he may have trouble with the state authorities responsible for its enforcement. Probably he would win such a dispute, but it might be expensive. On the other hand, if he obeys such a state law, he may very well be held for a state or federal EEOC violation. In the event that such a conflict in the law appears to exist in a particular state, good legal advice as to what course to follow is essential.

Certain patterns often found in the hospitality industry may present questions. For example, are maids exclusively women, while parking attendants, supervisory personnel, bartenders, and busboys are always men? If a woman is rejected for one of the "men's jobs" or a man for one of the "women's jobs,"[1] a complaint may be registered, and the employer will have to show that the patterns resulted from valid criteria not related to discrimination.

Even after management has assured itself that its hiring policies are not subject to criticism, other questions remain. A potentially serious problem is present when not only are there clearly defined men's and women's jobs, but also there is a pay differential between them that cannot be objectively

---

1. Except when a BFOQ can be established, as noted above.

CHAPTER 13

The Occupational Safety and Health Act (OSHA)

Introduction

IN APRIL, 1971 a new act of Congress became effective which had the broad objective of reducing job-related deaths, accidents, and health hazards. In the words of the Act itself, the purpose of this new legislation is:

". . .to assure so far as possible every working man and woman in the Nation safe and healthful working conditions and to preserve our human resources. . ."

The Act is designed to correct a real problem. The best estimates are that annually we experience about 14,000 job-related deaths and two million injuries. Exact figures are impossible to determine for the simple reason that no consistent, mandatory, reporting requirements were in force prior to the adoption of OSHA, a deficiency that has been corrected.

OSHA applies to practically every business concern in the United States, and it is difficult to imagine a member of the hospitality industry that would be excepted. The requirements of this Act are numerous, technical, and detailed. The penalties for non-compliance are severe. It is essential that every hospitality manager consider the implications of this Act in his own operation.

Administration

Administration of the Act was assigned to the Secretary of Labor. However, operations were delegated to the Assistant Secretary of Labor for Occupational Safety and Health, and an administrative agency created to handle the actual details of the Act. This agency is the Occupational Safety and Health Administration, abbreviated, as is the Act itself, OSHA. OSHA is a decentralized agency employing about 4,000 inspectors, who are the officials with whom the businessman is most likely to come into contact. Two-thirds of OSHA employees are in the field, operating out of 10 regional offices.

Section 5A of OSHA provides that each employer:

(1) Shall furnish to each of his employees employment and a place of employment which are free from recognized hazards that are causing or are likely to cause death or serious physical harm to his employees

(2) Shall comply with the occupational safety and health standards promulgated under this act

Paragraph (1) is referred to as the general duty standard, and it may be invoked in the event a hazardous condition is discovered, even though no specific standard is violated. It is in effect a catch-all, evidently designed to protect against dangerous situations overlooked in the specific standards. However, it has not been used by the administrators of OSHA to a very marked degree.

To find a violation of the general duty clause, it must be shown that a hazard was recognized as being dangerous by the industry involved. The OSHA compliance manual states that a hazard is recognized as dangerous when it is commonly considered to be so by members of the industry, not just by experts in the industry, and when the danger is detectable by means of the senses (e.g., sight, smell). Moreover, the probability of injury resulting from the danger must be more than merely remote.

The specific standards referred to in paragraph (2) are complex and multitudinous. There are several classifications of standards, some of which will not be discussed here. However, two classes of standards will be mentioned. First, horizontal standards, which embrace all industry groups and, therefore, are of interest to every employer. Horizontal standards refer to such activities as housekeeping, sanitation, noise, storage, and use of flammables. Second, vertical standards apply within a trade or industry. Hence, the only vertical standards the manager need be concerned with are those that have been adopted for his type of business concern; these will be discussed in the "Management Ideas" at the end of the chapter.

Inspection

How are these standards enforced? Most of the employees of OSHA are inspectors, who have experience in the particular industry for which they have the responsibility of inspecting and who have completed an OSHA-administered training course.

Inspectors are required to present themselves in a reasonable manner at regular working hours and to present their credentials. An employee, normally designated by the union, but who may be selected by the inspector if no other selection has been made, will usually accompany the inspector and the management representative in the "walk-around." Employees may bring complaints to the inspector if they wish. At the end of the inspection, the inspector will hold a conference with the employer and advise him of any violations.

If there have been violations noted, the inspector reports these to his area office, and the area office after reviewing the violation may send a citation. This must come within a reasonable time (the framers of the act considered 72 hours reasonable, but probably a somewhat longer period is within reason).

Agency Procedure

These citations have often been compared with an ordinary traffic citation. Each citation contains a named sum of money, which if paid terminates the issue just as does forfeiting bond on a traffic ticket. If the employer does not wish to "bond out," there is a procedure whereby he may fight the charge. Notice that the employer wishes a hearing must be sent to the area director within 15 days. A hearing will subsequently be held in the nearest locality that can provide adequate courtroom facilities, before a hearing examiner of OSHA.

Should the employer lose before the hearing examiner,

there is a possibility, but only a possibility, that the case might be reviewed before the 3-man board of OSHA. The statute provides that if one member of the board wishes the case to be heard before the full board (a re-hearing), the full board will review the case.

Otherwise, the decision of the hearing examiner will be the final disposition by the agency.

Following the final decision by the agency, an aggrieved party may still seek judicial review from the Federal Circuit Court of Appeals. However, as was stated in the chapter on Administrative Agency, judicial review is far from a new trial. The all-important findings of fact made by OSHA will normally be accepted, as, ordinarily, will be the standards and rules adopted by OSHA. The principal area of review by the court will be in the interpretations of law by OSHA, and if the review is not primarily over questions of legal interpretation, it is probably hopeless.

Violations

The citations may be of three types, depending upon the seriousness of the violation.

1. De minimis: if the violation is of a standard which has no immediate or direct relationship to safety and health. There is no penalty for this type of violation.

2. Not serious: some danger to health or safety, but not likely to cause serious physical harm.

3. Serious: if the danger presents a substantial probability of physical injury or death.

Abatement (removal of the dangerous condition) may be required as well as payment of a fine. Failure to take steps necessary to achieve abatement may result in a daily fine until compliance is achieved.

Penalties can be very severe under the supervision of OSHA. They are as follows:

1. Willful violations: Maximum $10,000 fine.

2. Willful violations causing death:

First violation: Maximum $10,000 fine plus six months in jail.

Second violation: Maximum $20,000 fine plus one year in jail.

3. Serious violations: Maximum $1,000 fine.

Based on considerations, including previous history, size

of business, good faith, etc., fine may be reduced up to 50 percent.

4. Non-serious violations: Same as above.

Management Ideas: Employee Safety[1]

1. The Occupational Safety and Health Act still contains some disputed areas, but it would be wise for management to observe all regulations—disputed or not disputed.

2. Keep a log on all occupational injuries and illnesses as well as supplementary records on the same. (See pp. 190 and 191.)

3. Post information on the Act in your hospitality operation in the area where employees usually report to work.

4. Management cannot discharge an employee because he filed a complaint or testified against you.

A safety committee, made up of sub-department heads, should be established to review past employee accidents in order to make preventive suggestions. The committee would also establish procedures for reporting known hazards to management. This group should be coordinated by the insurance carrier engineer and chaired by a conscientious junior executive.

Here are some other regulations concerning the work areas and access to them:

5. Swinging doors must have openings or windows made from safety glass or otherwise protected, and a work area must not be in the arc of a swinging door.

6. Certain slopes require either stairways, ramps, or ladders.

7. Provide a dumbwaiter if the height of the food preparation area is more than five steps from the height of the service area.

8. The kitchen area must be designed in such a way that it provides safe exits in case of emergency; the exits must be clearly marked and identified.

9. Provide training for new kitchen employees in the following areas: lighting gas- or oil-fired stoves; operating microwave cooking units; using cutlery and kitchen equipment; working

---

1. It is obviously beyond the scope of this text to present a complete enumeration of all the regulations of the Act in detail. Therefore, a broad discussion of the main areas will follow.

FORM III

OSHA No. 101
Case or File No. ------------

Supplementary Record of Occupational Injuries and Illnesses

Form approved
OMB No. 44R 1453

EMPLOYER

1. Name ---

2. Mail address --
   (No. and street)   (City or town)   (State)

3. Location, if different from mail address --

INJURED OR ILL EMPLOYEE

4. Name -- Social Security No. ------------
   (First name)   (Middle name)   (Last name)

5. Home address --
   (No. and street)   (City or town)   (State)

6. Age ------------ 7. Sex: Male------------ Female------------ (Check one)

8. Occupation --
   (Enter regular job title, *not* the specific activity he was performing at time of injury.)

9. Department --
   (Enter name of department or division in which the injured person is regularly employed, even
   though he may have been temporarily working in another department at the time of injury.)

THE ACCIDENT OR EXPOSURE TO OCCUPATIONAL ILLNESS

10. Place of accident or exposure --
    (No. and street)   (City or town)   (State)

    If accident or exposure occurred on employer's premises, give address of plant or establishment in which
    it occurred. Do not indicate department or division within the plant or establishment. If accident oc-
    curred outside employer's premises at an identifiable address, give that address. If it occurred on a pub-
    lic highway or at any other place which cannot be identified by number and street, please provide place
    references locating the place of injury as accurately as possible.

11. Was place of accident or exposure on employer's premises? ------------ (Yes or No)

12. What was the employee doing when injured? --------------------------------
(Be specific. If he was using tools or equipment or handling material,
name them and tell what he was doing with them.)

13. How did the accident occur? --------------------------------
(Describe fully the events which resulted in the injury or occupational illness. Tell what
happened and how it happened. Name any objects or substances involved and tell how they were involved. Give
full details on all factors which led or contributed to the accident. Use separate sheet for additional space.)

OCCUPATIONAL INJURY OR OCCUPATIONAL ILLNESS

14. Describe the injury or illness in detail and indicate the part of body affected. --------------------------------
(e.g.: amputation of right index finger
at second joint; fracture of ribs; lead poisoning; dermatitis of left hand, etc.)

15. Name the object or substance which directly injured the employee. (For example, the machine or thing
he struck against or which struck him; the vapor or poison he inhaled or swallowed; the chemical or ra-
diation which irritated his skin; or in cases of strains, hernias, etc., the thing he was lifting, pulling, etc.)
----

16. Date of injury or initial diagnosis of occupational illness --------------------------------
(Date)

17. Did employee die? -------------- (Yes or No)

OTHER

18. Name and address of physician --------------------------------

19. If hospitalized, name and address of hospital --------------------------------

Date of report -------------- Prepared by --------------------------------
Official position --------------------------------

with hazardous chemicals, and wearing slip-proof footwear.

10. All work areas including storerooms must have a minimum clearance.

11. When coffee urns are used, are manually filled, and exceed a specific height, a fixed or portable platform covered with a non-slip material has to be provided.

12. All walk-in refrigerators and freezers must have an opening device on the inside.

13. All passageways in work areas must have a minimum width and be free of obstructions.

14. Counter and table counters, where exposed to contact by employees when serving food and beverage, must be well rounded. (Use a nickel as reference.)

15. All equipment should be installed, maintained, and used according to approved safety practices (e.g., use guards with meat slicers—not the hand to hold the products).

16. Have the proper fire fighting equipment available; designate permanent areas for it; keep the access to it free, and instruct your employees in the proper use of it.

17. Train employees (male and female) to properly lift and carry heavy objects.

18. Floors should be kept dry and free of slipping and tripping hazards.

19. Furnish and use safety devices and safeguards and adopt practices, means, methods, and processes to provide a safe working place, e.g., grounding of all electrical equipment, guards on mechanical equipment.

20. If employees report unsafe equipment or methods or conditions, see to it that each is immediately remedied. Remember that they can file a complaint against you. Excessive noise brought about by today's musical entertainment is an unsafe condition for cocktail waitresses, bartenders, musicians, etc. Insist on proper decibel ratings.

21. The work area should be kept clean, sanitary, properly ventilated, and well illuminated.

Certain measures are contested, such as the installation of dumb waiters in existing facilities or the rounding of tables.

Check your state regulations to see if there exist any "grand-father clauses" which might offer you temporary relief.

Another important part of OSHA deals with the sanitary conditions of work places. Since it is so closely related to guests' foodservice sanitation, and in order to avoid duplication, the subject was covered in chapter 6, "Liability Based on Food or Beverage that Is Contaminated, Spoiled, Adulterated, or Contains Foreign Objects."

Epilog

This text has been written for the practitioner in the hospitality industry. It provides a management guide to a number of operational situations which have the potential for resulting in undesirable legal actions. Aside from the fact that large sums of money might be at stake, legal actions, in many instances and especially in smaller operations, have a tendency to disrupt the normal operational process. The manager or owner has to spend time attending to the legal problem, time which he could otherwise devote to his business; employees are questioned, written statements are taken, employees might even have to appear in court. Finally, the undecided legal issue may have a negative influence on the behavior of management, as a dark cloud influences our behavior when on a mountain hike.

The prudent manager will build our "Suggestions" into his operational procedures; they will become part of his written instructions to subordinates. He should not make the mistake of merely committing his instructions to paper. An active communication process should be set in motion by management to make employees both aware of the instructions and willing to accept the content.

Our industry suffers from one major ailment: high employee turnover. This means that the training process never stops. For that reason, appropriate training devices have to be available to provide continuous training without absorbing the supervisors' time: for example, written materials and slide shows. It is obvious that the new employee is more likely to jeopardize the legal position of an operation than an established employee, because of the former's lack of information. It is, therefore, especially important to provide new personnel with the appropriate information.

There is one other point which we have tried to stress, and this deals with the legal process. The emphasis of the text is on avoiding legal complications.

The text is in no sense a substitute for legal advice. The prudent manager will do everything in his power to prevent legal complications. If, despite determined efforts, a complication has developed, he or she should not try to handle it personally but should immediately call for legal advice: one book does not make one a lawyer. Since this is a management text, a manager should become familiar with many of our "Suggestions" and after a short while should be able to properly protect his operation by applying them where needed.

It is in this spirit that we have pooled our specialized knowledge and presented this material to the hospitality industry.

Glossary

Agency: The relationship resulting when an agent is authorized to act for a principal.

Agent: A party designated to conduct some legal relationship, usually forming contracts, for another party known as the principal.

Apparent Authority: A term used in the law of principal and agent. It means that while an agent does not have real authority, he nonetheless has the power to bind his principal because the principal created an appearance to third parties causing them to believe the agent did have power to act.

Arrears: Being behind in one way or another, usually having failed to make payments on time.

Assault: The tort designed to protect one from being placed in fear of impending attack. Concerned with *intent*, the essence is an offer or attempt to commit violence upon the victim.

Bailee: The party in possession of goods under a bailment relationship.

Bailment: The legal relationship which arises when one person has control and custody of the property of another.

Bailor: The owner of bailed property.

Battery: The tort designed to protect one from physical attack. The requirements are an intentional, unpermitted contact of any sort.

Careless Conduct: Any conduct which fails to meet the socially accepted notions of safety toward others on their property.

Civil Liability: An infraction of some aspect of our civil (i.e., non-criminal) law which exposes the party involved to being successfully sued.

Common Law: The body of legal precedents derived solely from court decisions. Beginning in medieval England, courts have continued to decide cases in vast areas of the law where no statutes have been enacted. This process continues today, and important areas of the law (for example, tort and contract) continue to be shaped mainly by common law. Today, the appellate decisions of our state courts determine the substance of our common law.

Contract: A voluntary agreement entered into between two parties; a contract is legally enforceable at law through a civil suit.

Criminal Liability: Violation of the criminal law resulting in the possibility that the party allegedly guilty of the violation may be prosecuted by the State.

Defamation: A generic term including both the torts of libel and slander. Both of these involve protection to reputation, and this term may be used if there is no reason to distinguish between written and oral injury to reputation.

Eviction: The process of removing a party from the premises he occupies.

Express Authority: A term used in the law of principal-agent. It means that an agent has real authority, which stems from verbal communication.

Gross Negligence: A high degree of negligence, most commonly involved in the law of bailments. When a bailment is for the sole benefit of the bailor, the bailee is not liable for ordinary acts of negligence but remains liable for extreme, or gross, negligence.

Guest: A party accepted for a stay at an inn. Guests are normally transient, residing at an inn only for a short stay, under circumstances where most facilities necessary for a short stay (such as maid service) are provided. Many important legal consequences discussed elsewhere in this text stem from the host-guest relationship.

Hospitality Operation: This rather recently established term includes hotels; motels; restaurants; taverns; foodservice operations, such as are found in colleges, hospitals, and industrial plants; and the many kinds of clubs.

Host: In effect, the role of the inn when it admits a guest. The host-guest relationship presupposes that the guest meets the requirements discussed above (see Guest) and that the inn provides services necessary for the temporary stay of the guest. The duty to accept guests is imposed upon the inn by law.

Implied Authority: A term used in the law of principal-agent. It means that an agent has real authority, but this authority stems from circumstances or acts rather than verbal communication. (See Express Authority and Real Authority.)

Inn: Hotels and motels which provide transient housing to travelers.

Innkeeping: Managing hotels or motels.

Innkeeper: The manager of a hotel or motel.

Jury: A body of impartial citizens impaneled by a court for the purpose of deciding the facts in a law suit. Normally, juries consist of 12 members but in some states and in some instances, 6-man juries are authorized.

Legal Authority: The statutes or common law cases or both which support a particular rule of law.

Libel: The tort designed to protect one from written or permanently recorded attacks upon character.

Lien: A legal hold on property. For example, a mortgage is a lien on property, so that if payments owing are not paid, the lien may be foreclosed, and the money recovered from a sale of the property.

Litigation: A law suit. Involvement in a legal action.

Negligence: The most common tort. Negligence may be found when a party fails to exercise reasonable care, and this failure results in injury to some other party.

Plaintiff: The party who initiates a law suit.

Principal: Generally, any party capable of forming legal relations, but more specifically a party who designates an agent to act on his behalf, usually to make contracts.

Real Authority: A term used in the law of principal-agent. It means that an agent actually has been granted the authority—either express or implied—he claims to have.

Slander: The tort designed to protect one from oral attacks upon character.

Statute: A rule of law enacted by the legislature. A particular piece of legislation.

Suit: The process of being involved in legal action. When plaintiff sues defendant, a suit is then involved.

Tort: A legal action based on wrongful conduct of defendant, and not based upon contract. Some of the more common torts are negligence, assault and battery, false imprisonment, and libel and slander.

INDEX

ABOUT THE AUTHORS

Jon P. McConnell is a Professor at Washington State University, where he has served on the faculty since 1957. A member of the bar, Dr. McConnell was educated at the University of Colorado and Millikin University, and received the degree of Doctor of Jurisprudence at Willamette University College of Law. He has written numerous articles for legal journals.

Lothar A. Kreck is Director of Hotel and Restaurant Administration at Washington State University, and a consultant to airlines, clubs, hotels, restaurants, and resorts. He received his law degree from the University of Denver. Dr. Kreck has held a variety of positions in the hotel and restaurant industry in Germany, Switzerland, the United Kingdom, Sweden, Canada, and the United States.